Which Language?

Diversification and the National Curriculum

Edited by David Phillips

Hodder & Stoughton

LONDON SYDNEY AUCKLAND TORONTO

British Library Cataloguing in Publication Data
Which language? diversification and the national curriculum.
   1. Great Britain. Secondary schools. Curriculum subjects.
   Languages. Teaching
   I. Phillips, David, *1944 Dec. 15–*
   407'.1241

   ISBN 0 340 51005 6

First published 1989

Typeset by Wearside Tradespools, Fulwell, Sunderland
Printed in Great Britain for the educational publishing division of
Hodder and Stoughton Ltd, Mill Road, Dunton Green, Sevenoaks,
Kent by Page Bros (Norwich) Ltd.

Contents

Notes on contributors

Michael Calvert is a Teacher Fellow at the Language Teaching Centre, University of York. During his time in York he has been involved in materials production as co-author of *¡Vaya!* and has participated in many aspects of the initial and in-service training work of the department. He is currently working on producing INSET materials and organising courses to help teachers to prepare for diversification.

After teaching for two years at the bilingual University of Fribourg/Freiburg in Switzerland **Dr Georgina Clark** was elected Laming Travelling Fellow at Queen's College, Oxford (1981 to 1983). Since 1984 she has taught German and French in maintained secondary schools; she joined the Oxford Project on Diversification of First Foreign Language Teaching (OXPROD) team in September 1988. She has published and undertaken research in two distinct fields, twentieth century German and Austrian theatre and the teaching of the German language. In addition she contributes regularly to teaching materials in support of BBC radio programmes for schools language courses. Most recently she is joint author with David Phillips of OXPROD's first Occasional Paper: *Attitudes Towards Diversification: results of a survey of teacher opinion*, 1988 (Oxford University Department of Educational Studies).

Caroline Filmer-Sankey, an experienced teacher of modern languages in comprehensive schools, has been undertaking research on aspects of the teaching of languages other than French since 1985; she is currently Research Officer for OXPROD.

Dr Geraint Wyn Jones is a lecturer in the School of Education at the University College of North Wales, Bangor. His research and teaching interests include the theory and practice of modern language teaching and bilingualism and bilingual education. His most recent publications are: *Profion Bangor* (Co-editor, 1986), a volume of diagnostic Welsh reading tests, and *Y Stori Fer a'r Stori Fer Hir* (1988), an introduction to the *conte* and *nouvelle* for sixth form and higher education students. During the 1988–1989 academic year he undertook a study of the intensive language learning centres recently established in North-West Wales.

Dr David Phillips is a Fellow of St Edmund Hall, Oxford, University Lecturer in Educational Studies, and Tutor in German at the Department of Educational Studies of the University of Oxford. His research and teaching interests are in two distinct fields: the theory and practice of modern language teaching, and the post-war history of education in Germany, particularly higher education. He is the author or editor of several books and articles in these areas, most recently *Languages in Schools: From Complacency to Conviction* (1988), as well as of school textbooks for the teaching of German. He is also General Editor of the *Oxford Review of Education*. He currently directs the Oxford Project on Diversification of First Foreign Language Teaching (OXPROD), funded by the Leverhulme Trust.

Dr Bob Powell has been Lecturer in Education (modern languages) in the School of Education at the University of Bath since 1976. Previous teaching posts included Lecturer in Italian at the University of Wales and Head of a large languages department in a comprehensive school in the Midlands. His main area of research has been gender differences in foreign language learning. He is the author of *Boys, Girls and Languages in School*, published by CILT in 1986. In the field of Italian teaching he has written two BBC beginners' courses: *Get by in Italian* (1981) and *When in Italy* (1989). He also scripted the BBC radio series *L'Italia dal vivo*, first broadcast in 1984. He is co-author of *Mastering Italian 2*, published by Macmillan in 1989.

Robert Pullin is Lecturer in Education (Russian and French) at the University of Sheffield. His main area of research interest is the teaching of Russian and the development of new teaching methods and materials. He is co-author of Part 2 of *Pervy Dialog*. He is currently developing a collaborative research project with the Institute of General Pedagogy of the USSR Academy of Pedagogical Sciences on teacher satisfaction. He was formerly Chairman and President of the Association of Teachers of Russian, is currently a member of the CILT Board of Governors, and co-directs, with David Rix, the York–Sheffield Russian Project. He has recently been appointed to the National Curriculum Working Group for Modern Foreign Languages.

David Rix is Lecturer at the Language Teaching Centre, University of York, and Tutor in Russian and French on the PGCE course there. His main area of research interest is language teaching methodology and the development of Russian language teaching materials. He was formerly Director of the Nuffield/ Schools Council Modern Languages Project, and more recently co-author of *Pervy Dialog*, produced in collaboration with the Pushkin Institute, Moscow. In 1986 he was awarded the Pushkin Medal for his services to Russian teaching by the International Association of Teachers of Russian, and was President of the Association of Teachers of Russian in 1987/88. With Robert Pullin he is co-director of the York–Sheffield Russian Project.

Sonia Rouve is Lecturer in Education and Tutor in charge of Romance Languages at the Centre for Educational Studies, King's College, University of London. Her research and teaching interests are in two related domains: linguistics applied to language teaching and the promotion of the teaching of Spanish. She is the author of several articles in these areas, e.g. *La enseñanza del español en el Reino Unido – dificultades y perspectivas* (1988), as well as of a range of teaching materials, most recently *En directo desde España* (1989). She is a frequent speaker, in Britain and abroad, on all aspects of the teaching of modern foreign languages. She is currently (1989) Chairman of the Association of Teachers of Spanish and Portuguese.

Farzana Turner was until recently an advisory headteacher with responsibility for community languages and bilingual education in Oxfordshire, where she led a team of bilingual and community language teachers working at all stages of schooling in the county. She has taught in primary and secondary schools and has been involved in in-service courses for both community language and mainstream teachers. Following a period of secondment to the University of Nottingham, where she was directing a European Community-funded project on Linguistic Diversity in Primary Schools (LDIP), she was appointed to her present post of Inspector for Multicultural Education in Northamptonshire.

David Westgate is a lecturer in Education at the University of Newcastle upon Tyne, where he is involved in both initial and in-service training as well as classroom research. His interest in foreign languages, and French in particular, belongs to a general fascination with language and its role in different kinds of classroom. His publications include *Investigating Classroom Talk* (1987), written with A D Edwards, and papers on aspects of classroom interaction, language teaching and teacher training. He has for several years collaborated with teachers at a local comprehensive school, researching interaction and communication in foreign language lessons.

Introduction:
The Realities of
Diversification

David Phillips

> There is nothing in the nature of a language other than French or in its teaching context that makes it either more or less feasible than French as first foreign language in a secondary school; there is nothing intrinsically associated with the language or its teaching that makes it likely to be either more or less successful than French if introduced as the first language. Many of the problems referred to by schools in our enquiry were exactly the problems raised by schools where French is the first foreign language: the prevalence of double periods on the time-table, insufficient frequency of contact, difficulty of setting, hostile or unsympathetic options systems and so on. On the other hand, good organisation, commitment and good teaching produced the same happy results with a language other than French as they do with French. [a]

Those modern linguists – among whom I count myself – who have been arguing for many years for a policy of diversification of first foreign language provision in our secondary schools, could not have foreseen the rapid progress that is currently transforming the position of languages other than French on the curriculum. Even a few years ago the notion of a government not only unlocking the gate to the 'secret garden' of the curriculum but actually trampling on the well-established, if haphazardly planted, flower beds discovered there, was unthinkable.

Whatever we may feel about the ways in which the present Government is transforming educational provision at all levels, there is general delight among linguists that at last a proper policy for foreign language provision has emerged. While we must be very concerned about the prospects for the *second* foreign language – to recommend a start delayed until Year 4 fails to appreciate the needs of many school language learners and the nature of changes in public examinations – the prospect of widespread diversified provision in Year 1 provides a challenge which most linguists are prepared to face with enthusiasm and commitment.

> The predominant position of French among the languages taught in English secondary schools has for many years been noted, often with regret. More recently it has been suggested that a number of factors (the introduction of primary school French, comprehensive reorganisation, the establishment of two-tier systems) have militated against the survival, let alone the expansion of other languages. [b]

I have sketched the development of policy for modern language teaching elsewhere[1] and Georgina Clark provides in this present volume further analysis of the steps by which the present position has been reached. Diversification itself, of course, is not new – not much in education is – and the arguments heard today can be traced back, as Georgina Clark shows, to the early years of the century. Throughout this Introduction I have interspersed quotations from various sources dating from 1914 to 1988. Readers might wish to try to date each of them and to check their results with the list given at the end. Many of the present arguments have a distinct air of *déjà vu* about them when seen in the context of nearly a century of debate about the nature of foreign language provision in schools.

> Provision of second foreign languages and alternative first foreign languages is, then, at best unsystematic and at worst haphazard. There are few signs of proper local policy, let alone regional or national consensus, except in so far as the complacent acceptance of the *status quo* can be regarded as policy. [c]

The same arguments have been trotted out, then, over a long period: trade links, historical and cultural links, numbers of speakers of particular languages throughout the world, holiday destinations of Britons, etc. There is also the complex question of language difficulty, addressed by several contributors to the present book. Supposing that it could be shown that most children would find language X more 'accessible', i.e. easier in the most general terms, than language Y, it would clearly make sense for that fact to be taken into account in deciding which language to teach. Quotation 'g' below touches on this issue, though from a different perspective, in suggesting that if the acquisition of learning skills is the main reason for studying a foreign language at school (not a reason heard much more than *sotto voce* from 'official' sources these days) then it does not matter which language is studied. But it would of course make sense for a supposedly *easier* language to be studied rather than one perceived to present major problems for English speakers. It would be sensible to promote language X rather than language Y in order to ensure the success on which continuing motivation to learn depends. Language X might become what Eric Hawkins has termed an 'apprenticeship' language.

It has always been possible for schools to teach German to some pupils in the first year since many language teachers are qualified in both French and German. A measure of diversity in language teaching could therefore be brought about immediately by offering German to a greater number of pupils than at present in the first year of their secondary course. Opinion varies as to the relative difficulty of German in the early stages, but the difficulties may appear greater to teachers who adopt a more traditional, analytical approach than to those who pursue a policy aimed at giving the pupils experience of the living language by aural-oral methods. [d]

Note that no one declaims violently against Spanish, German or Italian: that would probably provoke a strong reaction in their favour and do them more good than harm. The procedure is just to smile upon them and keep them quiet by saying condescendingly nice things about them – in other words, to inoculate education with a tiny dose of them so that it may never catch them badly. [e]

In the Oxford Project on Diversification of First Foreign Language Teaching (OXPROD), we have found that there is some evidence, as Caroline Filmer-Sankey puts it in the present volume, that 'first-year pupils are more positive about German than French in terms of their enjoyment, their perceptions of its difficulty and their desire to have contact with Germany and German-speaking people'. Elsewhere it has been reported that 'the highest proportions of both girls and boys finding the foreign language easy and enjoyable, was among pupils learning German'.[2] It is difficult to go beyond such statements; indeed, objective data on difficulty would be far from easy to obtain, unless we had at our disposal large numbers of children across a range of different abilities studying two languages, in various combinations, in parallel. Only then, and assuming that variables such as learning conditions (including the teacher) could be neutralised, could any objective *comparative* findings be even tentatively reached. It would be foolish, however, to ignore the subjective evidence on language difficulty which can be collected from both teachers and pupils. Papers on individual languages in this collection address some of the issues involved here.

The traditional liberal education in England is based on the Classics, French, and Italian. I suppose the railways killed Italian, with so many other good things, when the Grand Tour gave place to Messrs. Cook; and French only survived because of its diplomatic use, aided, no doubt, by its literature and the importance of France in the world of ideas. German then forced its way in because the Germans were important in politics and commerce. As a language, few but enthusiasts would claim much for it, and its literature cannot be compared with Italian. I hope a case may be stated at last for Italian instead of German. For business men, again, Spanish is even now more important than German. [f]

The question of which foreign language to teach centres usually on a decision between modern European languages. But the United Kingdom is a multilingual country, with a large number of so-called 'community languages' represented among its minorities of various ethnic origins. Such languages, especially Urdu, have often been introduced into the secondary curriculum, and not only for the benefit of those whose first language they are. It has been argued that community languages should be treated on a par with other (European) languages, but for some time it appeared that the Government would be restricting the choice to the major languages of Europe.

> An unfortunate feature of school provision in this country is generally considered to be the outstanding strength of French as against all other languages. The competitors presumably are Spanish and German, not, except in isolated cases, immigrant-community languages such as Gujerati and Punjabi. All of us, I think, keep saying that it would be healthier if Spanish or German were more often the first foreign language in a school. This has indeed come across extensively in the DES consultation process, but I want to take myself, again speaking personally, a querying stance. [. . .] If the main aim of exposure [. . .] to a foreign language is the acquisition of learning skills, does this consideration matter? It is not as though a scatter of different foreign languages really offered individual pupils a choice of which language they could learn: brave things are sometimes said about movement between schools for different subjects, but what can be sustained in actuality may be pretty limited. And different practices across schools can of course make transfers between schools more disruptive. So, with regrets, especially as someone who likes French as a language less than some others, I am not very sure about this complaint. I would give more attention, I think, to the wider availability for more pupils of a second foreign language, and hope that no one is lost to language learning because faced first with French. [g]

However, in March 1989, when the contributions to this volume already existed in draft form, it was proposed to specify two groups of languages to be taught in secondary schools. The Secretary of State announced the Government's intention in the following terms:

> The first group will consist of the working languages of the European Community – Danish, Dutch, French, German, Modern Greek, Italian, Portuguese, Spanish – and maintained schools will be required to offer pupils the opportunity to study at least one of these. The second group will include non-EC languages – Arabic, Bengali, Gujerati, Hindi, Japanese, Mandarin and Cantonese Chinese, Punjabi, Russian, Turkish, Urdu. Maintained schools will be allowed, but not required, to offer one or more of these in addition to those in the first group, as the National Curriculum foreign language.[3]

Community languages, then, may now be studied provided there is an alternative choice available. Modern Hebrew has since been added to the second group.

> French has long held a dominant place in the curriculum. You will, of course, know the reasons – geographical, cultural, commercial, diplomatic and linguistic – why this has come about. I am not sure this has been of entirely unqualified benefit to generations of native English speakers, or for that matter in the best interests of French itself. At any rate we are convinced that there would be immense advantages if the other great languages now taught in schools – German, Spanish, Italian and Russian – were on offer to many more pupils. They would widen and enrich the range of cultural experience open to children; offer them a greater variety of linguistic and intellectual challenges; and lay a stronger foundation for the later learning of other less common languages. [h]

What is also interesting in the Government's proposals is the surprising range of European languages in the first group. Its composition can only be understood, of course, in political terms. The actual teaching of Danish, Dutch, Modern Greek and Portuguese will remain negligible despite the status now accorded to those languages. Their inclusion provides the clue to the Government's enthusiasm for diversification: it is politically desirable to be able to demonstrate to Britain's European partners that policy makers are serious about young Britons learning the languages of the European Community. Wider educational considerations, we may suspect, have played a less significant part in the decision. Russian is accorded less status than any of the other commonly taught European languages . . .

> The small amount of attention given to Russian studies in this country is entirely out of proportion to the importance of the Soviet Union in the world today [. . .] The educational value of Russian is as great as that of any other modern language [. . .] The immediate objective should be to bring the numbers studying Russian up to the numbers at present learning German. [i]

The Oxford project already referred to has been investigating organisational problems in a number of schools which already have diversified provision of first foreign languages. While there are some concerns about maintaining adequate staffing, we have found a remarkably positive response to the experience of diversification in the schools we have surveyed. Our first interim report concludes:

Languages were seen to be enjoying a high profile, staffing resources were being wisely deployed and there was little linguistic expertise in schools which was not being tapped. Only 9% of individual teachers were not in favour of diversification policies, the vast majority responding positively to the changes which diversification had brought about. [. . .] Problems were encountered, but they were not insurmountable. It is clear that the task of countering parental surprise or even displeasure when a language other than French is offered as first foreign language requires careful planning and advance PR work, but, reassuringly, initial parental concern is widely reported to dissipate once pupils are successfully launched on their study of the new language. [4]

Despite the positive findings in our limited survey, there are widespread concerns nationally about the number of extra teachers that will be needed if diversification is to become a reality in most local education authorities, and, indeed, if all children are to be taught a foreign language up to the age of sixteen. Estimates of the extra teachers required vary enormously, from 2,000 to 4,000, and it is clear that even if the Government's optimism about the potential availability of teachers already in the system with 'exploitable' qualifications is founded, such teachers will need urgent retraining.[5]

There are worrying teacher shortages in the United Kingdom in other subject areas too, and various *ad hoc* measures are being proposed to deal with them, including 'licensing' otherwise unqualified people to teach, and the provision of 'on-the-job' training. Such stop-gap measures, taken alongside recent Government initiatives which have seriously affected the nature of teacher training in colleges and universities, are seen by hard-pressed teachers and trainers as particularly unfortunate.

> What advice can we give, in the absence of a nationally agreed policy? It can only be to choose the course that has fewest disadvantages for a particular school. Ideally we would welcome the dual first foreign language pattern, with French offered every year to cater for the intake from feeder schools committed to French and late entries already embarked on French and in recognition of the present availability of French staffing. The choice of the second language in each year must lie between German and Spanish. It might be possible to offer German one year and Spanish the next as the language for half the intake. This would be the best solution if staffing and falling rolls permit. It is, however, most important in all this not to exaggerate the finality of whatever language choice a given pupil will make. The decision is not a life-or-death affair.[j]

Another matter which is of concern in the context of diversification is the possible effect of the arrangements for local management of schools. Head-teachers, who will still have considerable influence in curricular matters, might well regard the language(s) on offer in their schools as a potential selling-point to the parents of the locality. Already in one of the OXPROD schools there is a tendency to question the desirability of offering Spanish as parallel first foreign language, largely as a result of the head's fear of the potential lack of attraction his school might have among parents 'shopping around' for a good school. Schools 'opting out' under the provisions of the 1988 Education Reform Act might well be preoccupied with the same considerations *vis-à-vis* modern foreign language provision. In either case the safe option will be to resort to the *status quo ante*, and French will again dominate.

> To sum up, we think that, although a claim can be made both for the cultural and for the utilitarian value of any modern language, the traditional emphasis on French and German is still justified on educational grounds, though we would

gladly see some redressing of the balance in favour of German. None the less we believe that the claims of foreign languages other than French and German should be fully and generously met, especially those of Russian and Spanish. [k]

The independent schools, exempt from the provisions of the National Curriculum, will be able to continue to offer whatever combinations of languages they wish, to be started whenever they decide. With the expectation that under the terms of the National Curriculum the *second* foreign language will not be introduced until Year 4, maintained schools will be at a distinct disadvantage compared to their independent counterparts. It is the independent schools that will be producing the double linguists for whom many universities look.

It is clearly impossible to predict for any particular child what language he or she may need to use later in life. But we believe that if we could establish a broader language base among young people as a whole, that would also help our export effort. A number of studies have suggested that German and French are equally in demand by exporting companies and there is also a strong need for Italian and Spanish. There is, therefore, a strong case both economically and on broader educational and cultural grounds for widening the access to languages other than French in schools. [1]

The papers which follow present the case for the five most commonly taught European languages. There is always a tendency to polemicise when writing about subjects on which heart-felt views have been developed over many years; each contributor, however, as a specialist observer of the scene around each of the languages in question, presents the case with an infective enthusiasm rather than a ferocious bias, taking into account historical developments, current provision, and prospects for the future. Farzana Turner describes the position of community languages, and Geraint Wyn Jones traces policy development as it affects the teaching of Welsh. Finally, Caroline Filmer-Sankey, who has worked closely (within OXPROD) with the present editor and with Georgina Clark (whose analysis of policy development closes the discussion) provides a detailed account of research concerning language difficulty, attainment, and pupil attitude.

No doubt as a factor of the first magnitude in shaping the destiny of Europe during the last hundred years, Germany must retain a permanent and compelling interest to the historical student, though the estimate of the causes which have raised her to that position may undergo changes in the opinion of succeeding generations. And on this also there will be general agreement. After the war the importance of German must correspond with the importance of Germany. If Germany after the war is still enterprising, industrious, highly organised, formidable no less in trade than in arms, we cannot afford to neglect her or ignore her for a moment; we

> cannot leave any of her activities unstudied. The knowledge of Germany by specialists will not suffice; it must be widespread throughout the people. A democracy cannot afford to be ignorant.[m]

Morale among language teachers has not been high. While it is encouraging that policy frameworks for modern language teaching have been established, it is a matter of concern that the political dimension involved in reaching policy decisions has overridden the traditional British concern for the pragmatic dimension. As Mark Twain might have put it, once a politician gets his hands on a school subject, it's goodbye subject.

The British Government's policy statement on modern languages[6] states the utilitarian and political case for language learning in its opening paragraph, which refers to the nation benefiting economically and culturally from an ability to communicate with foreigners in their own language. Opportunities will be created in trade, tourism, international relations, science, and other areas, and Britain's effectiveness as a member of the European Community will be improved.

It is in the second paragraph that we find the arguments for language learning lifted above the level of the practical/utilitarian: here there is talk of 'insights into the nature of language and language learning', of contribution to 'an understanding of the cultures, attitudes and ways of life in other countries' which is of importance in international relations, of the promotion of 'a disciplined and active approach to learning and the satisfaction of gaining competence and understanding which are both rewarding and useful'.

The order in which those two groups of arguments relating to aims and objectives are listed is worrying if it is a symbol of notional priorities, just as the prioritising of the two groups of languages which may be included in the National Curriculum is a matter of concern to community language teachers and Russian specialists. But if the two sets of aims can be kept in view in all planning for the teaching of foreign languages (whatever languages), if the wider benefits of language learning are properly recognised alongside the utilitarian ones, we can then welcome unreservedly – as most modern linguists are inclined to do – the increased investment in modern foreign language teaching that present policy implies.

> LEAs and schools should ensure that a reasonable proportion of their pupils of all abilities study a language other than French as their first foreign language. Although it would be impossible to specify an ideal mix of language provision in schools, the current situation is clearly inappropriate to the needs of a modern trading nation. In trading terms alone, a number of studies suggest that German and French are equally in demand by exporting companies; and that there is also a strong need for Italian and Spanish.[n]

1

French – First among Equals?

David Westgate

What matters it how far we go? his scaly friend replied.
There is another shore, you know, upon the other side.
The further off from England the nearer is to France –
Then turn not pale, beloved snail, but come and join the dance.

(Lewis Carroll: Alice in Wonderland, 1865)

The Mock Turtle's song is truly Victorian, confident and expansionist. Appreciating that England, though an island, does have neighbours, he nevertheless looks first to France – naturally. He appears to be making an assumption common among his ancestors over the previous 800 years: that our closest cultural as well as geographical neighbours are the French. The idea that their language is also the natural one for a civilised Englishman to learn has since proved equally enduring.

For modern language teaching, the decade of Alice has another significance. It marks the beginning of an upsurge of interest in the teaching of languages which was to lead to their recognition as part of the curriculum of our schools. Hitherto, languages had been taught almost entirely outside them, conducted by native speakers acting as private tutors or employed in academies. The last thirty years of the nineteenth century were to witness a serious attempt to establish languages as respectable subjects worthy of inclusion within the 'Modern Sides' of the newer public schools and thereafter in the 'county' schools set up following the 1902 Education Act. Since the study of modern foreign languages needed to gain acceptance as a discipline equal in rigour to the Classics, it is understandable that the schools should turn first to the traditionally respected culture and language of France, and that they should teach these by concentrating upon grammar, translation and, eventually, literature.

These developments contain the first of many ironies concerning French teaching in Britain. Acceptance was gained at the cost of an obligation to abandon utilitarian aims which had previously gone unquestioned; French had temporarily to join the ranks of the 'dead' languages. The need at this time to avoid scornful dismissal as mere 'courier French' was to have profound and lasting effects upon the style as well as the status of French in the secondary curriculum. Viewed in this perspective, therefore, what stands out from the emergent policy concerning modern languages in the National Curriculum is that it should both challenge the dominant position of French and, for the first time, officially set practical communicative goals as the overriding priority for all school-based languages teaching.

It will be the purpose of this contribution to elaborate that perspective and to consider its consequences. First, the present dominance of French must itself be examined, to assess its strength and to account for its origins in more detail. It will then be possible to consider the curricular claims made specifically for French and to offer some pointers towards roles it can reasonably be expected to play within the new framework.

The dominance of French

> The majority of pupils currently learn French as their first foreign language. The reasons for this relate to tradition and the supply of teachers rather than to any intrinsic advantages possessed by French.[1]

The HM Inspectorate thus encapsulates both the facts of the present situation and a widespread professional attitude towards it. By criteria based on the proportion of candidates entering for public examinations in French and other foreign languages (FLs), as well as on the proportion of schools offering French as first foreign language (FL1), it is clear that for most pupils foreign language learning is confined to French.

Taking the examination entries first, it is clear from Figure 1 below that French enjoys (if that is the word) an overwhelming share.

Figure 1

FL examination entries, French and other FLs: GCE O Level/GCSE (16+) and GCE A Level (18+), 1986

	16+	18+
French	244,170 (72.2%)	16,810 (64.4%)
All other FLs	93,780 (27.8%)	9,300 (35.6%)

Source: *Statistics of Leavers, CSE and GCE*, 1986, pp. 17, 25 (DES)

Hawkins reminds us that these figures must be interpreted against a background of other changes over recent years. He usefully includes figures for the School Certificate, as taken in 1938, and demonstrates first a decline in entries for foreign languages as a proportion of entries in all subjects: from 16.3% in 1938 to 9.4% in 1965 and 6.6% in 1985. Over the same period, he is able to show that FLs other than French have gained slowly but consistently on French, in spite of the effects of the Primary French pilot scheme (1963–74).

Calculating non-French FL entries as a percentage of those for French, Hawkins charts the advance thus: 15.9% in 1938, 31.3% in 1965 and 33.7% in 1985. When 18+ examination entries are compared (Higher Certificate, 1938; A level, 1965 and 1985), the equivalent figures are 22%, 42.6% and 58% respectively. Hawkins summarises thus:

> Though the 'minority' languages continue to improve their position relative to French, the position of Modern Languages as a whole . . . becomes steadily weaker.[2]

The improvement is only relative, and French can still be justly described as 'entrenched'[3] when we take account of languages offered as FL1 in schools (see Figure 2).

Figure 2

Percentages of schools offering FL1 by language

Languages	%
French	90
German	21
Spanish	4

Source: Assessment of Performance Unit: *Foreign Language Provision*, p. 4, 1983 (DES)

Some schools offer more than one FL1 for 11 year olds to choose from (hence percentages totalling more than 100), but the overall lack of variety remains striking and regrettable. It is generally recognised that individual pupils vary in their tastes for and responses to different languages. Some evidence of variation by region and gender, for instance, was highlighted by Burstall et al.,[4] with northern pupils (and boys in particular) being less pro-French than their southern counterparts. Supporting evidence comes, too, from schools where pupils are offered a change of FL at, say, 13+; individual performance can vary from language to language either way. Also, since a second foreign language (FL2) is usually only offered from year three to those who have already demonstrated some aptitude in FL1, French is effectively acting as a screening device, limiting access for many who might have preferred, or done better in, a language other than French.

This 'hegemony' of French[5] is far from being the calculated creation of French teachers. Despite some lingeringly elitist associations of French with the high cultural fare of traditional (grammar school) teaching, it has in fact been the comprehensive teachers of French who more than those of other languages have been challenged to find ways of working with mixed-ability and low-ability classes in Years 1 to 3. Many of them would doubtless be happy enough to see this burden more evenly shared, the more so with pupils constrained to take a five-year course. They might happily take a share of self-selecting classes in the new Key Stage 4 (14–16).

The evident truth is that the dominance of French results from factors which have become self-confirming. Playing a key role is the supply and training of teachers. With the imbalance in secondary FL provision to some extent mirrored in higher education, there are naturally more graduate teachers of French. Figure 3 shows French still holding 68.6% of the training places.

Figure 3

Main FL offered by PGCE students, 1986–87

French	498
German	191
Spanish	26 (compared with 60 in 1974)
Russian	9 (30 in 1974)
Italian	2 (9 in 1974)

> N.B. Some offer a subsidiary language not shown;
> Joint Honours FL graduates included twice;
> total of students 687.

Training opportunities have also been reduced. In 1977, the B.Ed. with a specialism in FL (largely French) counted 1,151 students.[6] That route has now disappeared. PGCE numbers have also fallen in the decade from 911 to 687. A further drop of over 10% was reported for 1987 and is being compounded in recruitment for 1989. Hawkins and Lawrence find this situation 'supremely ironic'.

As firms prepare for new marketing opportunities in Europe from 1992, and as an increasing proportion of new graduates is drawn into careers more lucrative than teaching, it is hard to foresee teacher supply eroding this dominance of French. Industry will attract graduates of all languages, leaving the largest group, potential French teachers, even more preponderant. Reliance on foreign nationals queueing up to teach here or on a pool of mis-employed teachers of other FLs, begins to look seriously complacent. If the former were to occur, it would perhaps be as well to recall that employment of native speakers in the public and endowed grammar schools of the early nineteenth century was one important factor contributing to the low esteem in which languages were held there.

If 'a language for all' is not mostly to mean 'French for all', the teacher supply problem will require more imaginative consideration and more resources, directed not only at salaries but at training initiatives, initial and in-service, as well as at LEA support and research. Many FL teachers recall that the Primary French pilot scheme also foundered upon a shortage of adequately qualified personnel.[7] It had focussed exclusively on French, principally because of the teacher supply factor, anticipating that other FLs would enjoy increased opportunities in secondary schools from age 11. In the event, failure of the scheme caused these opportunities not to materialise; ironically, French became further entrenched as the FL1 which the secondary schools needed to offer for the sake of continuity.

Other factors, however, have played their part. As secondary school rolls have fallen in the 1980s, it has been hard for heads to preserve variety in languages taught. French has had tradition and convenience behind it. Teaching resources have been abundantly available, and the increasing mobility of pupils and their families across LEA boundaries has pointed curricular policy towards conformity. Some 'rival' languages, notably Russian, have suffered circumstantially. More generally, poor national motivation for FL study has failed to lend support to an enthusiastic branch of the profession whose work and subjects have too often been marginalised or treated as the 'sore-thumb' of the comprehensive curriculum[8] as well as being deemed 'difficult' by pupils. At least that situation now has official recognition and current policy is to be specifically aimed at remedies.[9] Signs of an increasing social awareness of languages and a recognition of their potential contribution,[10] are also emerging and may underpin the expansion essential to diversification. Since, however, diversification is only mentioned in the policy statement[11] and not in the Education Reform Act itself, there is a strong risk that the dominance of French will merely give way to a consolidation upon French-plus-one-other-FL (most probably German) as two parallel FL1 alternatives, with all others squeezed into 'minority time'.

The force of tradition

In his 'social history' of modern languages in the secondary curriculum in England, Radford[12] writes of four main phases. His first takes us from the Norman Conquest to the Napoleonic Wars. That phase saw French evolve from an upper-class to a foreign language, with English established as a consciously national language and Latin still used for much of this period in the business of state and church. It was essentially, too, the 'era of the private tutor when languages (principally French) were learned by the rich and ambitious from native speakers for practical purposes'.[13] With the mounting power and prestige of France under Louis XIV, the fashion for everything French reached a peak in England. But by the time of the Stuarts, mastery of standard French had already been, and was to remain until modern times, 'an indispensable passport to high society or a career in the diplomatic service for young men of rank'.[14] For young women, to speak French was a valued 'social accomplishment'.

Respect for French culture was to endure, although by the early nineteenth century revolution and wars had taken their toll. For a while France even became a feared enemy. Nevertheless, Radford's second phase of language teaching (lasting until 1914) was 'marked by the struggle for recognition in leading schools and universities, where modern languages were commonly despised as the poor man's Latin'.[15] At this time German began to rival French, still viewed by many as the source of dangerous ideas. From the 1870s on, both were involved in the delicately balanced competition between Classics and Moderns, as well as in that between academic and 'direct' teaching methods. However, war once again intervened.

By the 1920s German had lost ground to French and, in the years that followed, the methodological balance also continued to revert to the more neo-classical style. Not only had modern languages had to pay their price for respectability, but 'direct method' teaching had appeared ill-suited to the schools and had generally lost credit. Thus by the 1950s, languages had settled in as 'an essential part of the humanistic curriculum of which the selective schools were the guardians'.[16] 'Whitmarsh French' was ensconced in the grammar schools of an England which had 'never had it so good'.[17] This third period, then, from World War I to about 1960, saw languages expand and gain status. They were also to be underpinned by university-dominated public examinations even beyond the 'dynamic innovations of the sixties' which mark the beginning of Radford's final phase.

There was talk at that time of a 'revolution' in language teaching:

> Old methods, old objectives, old notions of language had been superseded, it was claimed, by altogether sounder ones based on science and technology . . . Certainly the new ideas had an impressive appearance and inspired more confidence than the Ancien Régime.[18]

Three factors can then be credited with influencing languages in general and French in particular. First, there was new technology with new concepts of language and habit-based learning. Second came comprehensive schools and the 'democratisation' of French teaching, lending further weight to utilitarian aims and objectives. The third centred on the relaxation by universities, as they competed for students in the post-Robbins era, of the requirement that all entrants have a modern language qualification.

The first did less than expected to make French more popular or effective. Students who were at secondary school in the 1970s speak with little more affection of Jean-Paul, Claudette and Marie-France[19] than their predecessors did of Whitmarsh and his works. Pupils consistently reported distaste for the 'tireless' tape-recorder and the spread of high achievement failed to materialise. Rumours of a 'crisis' in modern languages found apparent confirmation in HM Inspectorate's report of 1977,[20] and were echoed in the findings of DES/APU (1986).[21]

For French, the introduction of non-selective schools was even more significant. These not only became the context for the dominance of French already described; they were to pose questions about the viability of utilitarian goals across the ability range and hence about languages in the curriculum at all.

Abandonment of the FL requirement by higher education entailed what for many seemed a catastrophic loss of subsidiary (mostly French) pupils, even though it also opened up the possibility of practical studies for the majority. On this latter issue opinions divide. Hawkins, for instance, may be seen as one-time optimist turned pessimist. His metaphor of school-based FL teaching as 'gardening in a gale of English' strikingly identifies the difficulties of teaching French (etc.) in at best 10% of the available timetable.[22] Radford goes further, seeing the dethroning of grammar along with the schools to which it had lent its name, as risking a wholesale decline.

> The familiar association of low-status, skill-based learning and poor intellectual endowment was simply re-asserting itself: French ... was reverting to its pre-Victorian humble status as a useful accomplishment like handicraft.[23]

And there were plenty more who saw the whole FL enterprise as doomed if it had nothing but utilitarian goals to offer.

It is tempting to judge the pessimists' arguments against their pre-examination reform background and to side with the optimists who cite the achievements by the graded objectives schemes[24] and point especially to the impact of GCSE as legitimising new objectives and setting a different agenda for schools to work to. Certainly, the first signs have been encouraging, and more so in modern languages than in many other subjects. Yet the context remains in other respects unchanged; time, and especially resources, are still pressing constraints. There are also still tensions to resolve, for example between would-be 'authentic' teaching and examiners' strange fixation for unrealistically separated skills-testing in GCSE. Similarly, it is hard to be sure whether the 'new eclectism' in teaching methods[25] really does represent adoption of pragmatically tested procedures, or whether it reflects a more negative distrust of modish ideals and a flight from principle.

What was needed to coincide with the re-emergent optimism was a firm lead. This has been forthcoming in the National Curriculum legislation and the accompanying *Statement of Policy* – which has been largely welcomed:

> the great majority of pupils should study at least one foreign language throughout secondary education . . .

with more pupils studying FLs other than French and continuing beyond 16 where possible so that:

> standards of communication in foreign languages should be improved for pupils of all abilities.[26]

This development can be seen, *in the perspective of our national tradition*, as confirming a radical redirection of language teaching which puts French on its mettle.

The claims for French

In turning our attention now specifically to French, we shall need to bear in mind differences between the roles it may play as FL1 and FL2 and also differences between practical and more broadly educational aims. Although the practical-communicative aims now have official priority, the broader category will continue to represent for many the principal justification for including FLs in the curriculum. The categories are also interdependent: attitudes and confidence, for instance, are built up *through* positive practical experience, and failure may be linked with boredom or even embarrassment in FL lessons.[27] Teaching and classroom relationships must therefore not be forgotten as we attend to the intrinsic features (and difficulties) of French for English-speaking pupils.

So, can French *of itself* be described as a good choice for 11-year-old beginners? What does it entail for our practical and other aims?

A useful starting-point is the concept of 'linguistic distance'[28] by which the difficulty of a given target-language is held to derive from differences, at different levels (e.g. sound system or syntax), between it and the learner's mother tongue. French appears easier on some criteria, harder on others. Lexically, for instance, it poses fewer problems than it does in its grammar, or particularly its phonology and spelling. History accounts for a certain shared word-stock and less lexical distance between English and French (or other Romance languages) than between, say, English and Russian. This is mostly an advantage, but also involves the well-known *faux amis* syndrome: e.g. *décevoir* is *to disappoint*, not *deceive*. Problems of syntax can appear formidable. The gender system of French is essentially 'grammatical', rather than 'natural' (as English); gender is also very unreliably sign-posted by word-form: c.f. *garage* and *image*, *morceau* and *eau*, and mute *-e* endings. Some regularities do exist, but genders have mostly to be learned, and on that learning depends a host of other grammatical detail. For English pupils, too, the first tense encountered involves a mental compression of three English forms (*I watch/do watch/am watching*) into one; hence **Je suis regardant* and the like.

Intra-language differences compound the difficulties associated with inter-language ones. This is the case with French phonology and its relation to writing. The French sound-system includes consonants such as uvular [r] and word-final post-dental [l] as in *elle* (cf. English *bell*), which are unfamiliar to young English ears; also vowels which are not dipthongised as in English (c.f. *il* and *eel*; *site* and *seat*) and others which are strangely nasal (*pain, bon, an*). Then, in matching sounds to spellings, there appear, from an English standpoint, to be horrendous inconsistencies: e.g. endings to be sounded or not (*par, pars, part, pare* but *parc*) and many ways of representing a single sound (*é, et, ai, ez, er*).

In synthesising James's analysis, Hawkins places French fourth in an ascending order of difficulty, with Italian, Spanish and German easier and Russian harder.[29] James himself, however, subordinates 'distance' features to social, geographical and political factors, arguing that 'command of English and French goes further towards making one a "citizen of the world" than a combination of English with any other language'.[30] These views highlight our need to relate linguistic arguments to particular groups of pupils and the aims we set them.

'Distance' is more of an issue in choice of FL1 than of FL2: the more distant the less appropriate, perhaps. French appears to be something of an in-between case. For pupils aiming at basic communicative skills in French as FL1, early-stage difficulties do give pause for thought. Pronunciation, gender, and tenses, for example, all require careful teaching. Embarrassment over 'funny' sounds in French is often hard to avoid, particularly among adolescents in mixed classes. Such problems also attend some of our most able and best-intentioned public figures; and recently the hilarious policeman Crabtree, in television's *Allô! Allô!*, has raised our shameless mangling of French phonology to the level of a national joke. More familiar vocabulary and less familiar grammar may partly account for the fact that a proportion of pupils fail to get beyond one-word or set-phrase utterances. Writing difficulties, though evidently severe, can these days be minimised pre-16. On the other hand, French is not alone in presenting immediate problems (cf. case inflection in German) or difficulties unavoidable in a five-year course (cf. *ser* and *estar* in Spanish).

Two provisional conclusions can at any rate be drawn. First, the *inherent* case for French as FL1 is at best no stronger than that of some alternatives. Second, since all languages are by definition separate systems, to learn any one of them which is not too 'distant' will serve the very important function expected of all FL1 learning, namely 'apprenticeship' to the skills of language study itself, giving initial awareness of the kinds of inter-language differences which can occur.

Neither of the above points is readily inferable from the claims for their language made by many French nationals. As Harzic has written, *'Les Français ont une conviction innée de la supériorité de leur langue'*.[31] Woodhaugh[32] quotes one such eulogy, by Rebouillet;

> ... *les caractères privilégiés de cette langue. Rappelons-les: la clarté, la beauté, la perfection ... l'utilité ... la simplicité.*[33]

It is a familiar theme but one which conflicts with a simple maxim of linguistic science: '... that all languages are equally serviceable ... and that no language is inherently "better" or "worse" than any other language'.[34] Certainly much French writing is of great beauty but testifies to the quality of individual writers, not the language as a whole.

In any case, these abstractions transcend the broadest aims of the compulsory curriculum which have more to do with, for example, ear-training, confidence-building and the opening of young minds to the viability and attractiveness of other ways of talking and living. For such general educational purposes, pupils need teachers – of whatever FL – with skill, sensitivity and enthusiasm. Yet discussion of learners' needs often fails to give high priority to good teaching, even though there is now some relevant research into classroom skills to call upon, for example Sanderson's[35] follow-up of good practice identified by HMI,[36] Mitchell[37] and the Stirling project, Westgate et al.,[38] and others.

Frequently, too, discussion of 'needs' subordinates the quality of pupils' classroom experience to issues of national commerce. Arguments sometimes claim a need to provide instruction in the world's most widely spoken languages. (French comes a mere twelfth, whatever that may imply). More often considered are patterns of trade between the United Kingdom and other countries. Though it is possible to be too Euro-centric on social as well as commercial grounds, it appears to be true that much of our export business now involves countries where French and other main European languages are spoken. Our European markets have grown as others have declined. French has become relatively salient and the 1992+ integration will doubtless intensify that situation. Yet it also appears that British industry has been complacent about English as the world's main trading language and has shown a lack of concern about FL skills in the workforce.[39]

Thus the Government's lead in stressing an improved 'national capability' is no doubt timely:

> Compared with many trading nations, ours has a damagingly small proportion of people who understand and speak a modern foreign language.[40]

However, there is little official recognition of the fact that individual adults' FL needs are very unpredictable, or that the logic of national commercial arguments points to more general skills and attitudes: those which are needed for learning *any* FL when its imminent use is known. Language learning capacity is properly the business of schools but will not best be fostered by narrowly vocationalist aims (see, for example, Embleton[41]). The concern should be to provide a range of FLs catering for different tastes and to ensure that language learning is seen to be valued by being adequately resourced and well taught. The point is particularly relevant to French, which has suffered from being so often the only FL available and from being then blamed for putting off pupils who, naturally enough, can foresee few specific applications.

Some encouragement about attitudes can be found from schools where FLs have already become compulsory in the 11 to 16 curriculum.[42] Pupils are most positive about FL learning in those schools where HMI considered 'good quality' work to be going on.[43] Yet individuals' views varied widely, both towards FLs in general and towards particular languages according to their perceived difficulty. Disturbingly, too, French was seen as 'the most difficult compulsory subject' for average pupils.[44] Among the more able, boys found French harder than mathematics, while girls found it easier. Less able boys and girls found it hard and enjoyed it relatively little. Those learning German and Spanish rated languages as more enjoyable than the whole group did when French pupils were included. The pattern is familiar: French seen as hard, enjoyed more by girls than boys, and strongly associated with negative attitudes for many.

Conclusion

The contemporary status of French is not underpinned by commensurate arguments based on inherent advantages. Its relative unpopularity, particularly among boys, has not helped towards making practical FL command the widely valued aspiration it ought to be. Early-stage difficulties in French may in fact make it more suited to being offered as FL2, but that development is unlikely on a large scale. French will more probably retain a first-among-equals status, because it scores highly on key criteria: the proximity of France, the high profile of French in European politics and business, the abundantly available teaching and support materials, and especially the number of teachers qualified to teach it. French is also a language which, together with the people who speak it, their culture and beautiful country, continues to command special affection in many English hearts. If diversification were to mean French no longer being the single take-it-or-leave-it item on the FL menu in our schools, it might become more attractive and less of a scapegoat for our national linguistic chauvinism.

Chances for German

David Phillips

> No learned man doth now talk, or even so much as cough, save only in German [. . .]
> Now-a-days no man of science, that setteth any store by his good name, will cough
> otherwise than thus, *Ach! Euch! Auch!*[1]

Lewis Carroll's view, expressed with a haughty irony, that 'all that is good
comes from the German' and that men of science will agree 'that any German
book must needs surpass an English one' reflects, if it does not endorse, the
enthusiasm for the German language and for German culture that had developed
during the nineteenth century.

The German universities became magnets for British and American scholars
wishing to sit at the feet of distinguished German academics from Fichte,
Schelling and Hegel at the beginning of the century to Ranke, Mommsen, Lotze
and Wilamowitz at its end. Despite the high degree of competence in German
required to read the German philosophers, great efforts were made among the
educated classes to grapple with the spoken language. At Balliol under Jowett
speaking German became something of a modish affectation:

> Things that could have been more naturally said in English were sometimes
> deliberately said in German, as if it were a kind of superior argot.[2]

Although German had been unpopular under the Hanoverians, once Victoria
had succeeded to the throne and married Albert of Saxe-Coburg in 1840 the
language grew considerably in popularity, in spite of English speakers' difficulties with it. In 1876 it could be reported, with not a little exaggeration, that:

> In every school there are German governesses and masters; every little schoolmiss will
> rattle out her declensions for you, and be quite ready to air her German when her
> parents take her abroad for an autumnal trip.[3]

The rise of German militarism and the Anglo-German antagonism which
grew apace in the early years of the new century, seriously affected the public
perception of the language. Some years ago I discovered that a 1911 Bechstein
piano in my family's possession had had its brass lettering ('*Hof-Lieferant Sr.
Maj. des Kaisers u. Königs*') varnished over to expunge not only reference to the
Kaiser but all trace of the alien tongue.

The First World War created serious setbacks for the study of German in

Britain. But there is evidence that some educationists, though counselling caution, wished to see German continued. The Head Master of Plymouth College stated at a speech day in 1918 that:

> he did not think German would be of practical use after the war for commercial or personal intercourse. Either Spanish or Italian would provide as good a literary and linguistic training, though it would be a great mistake to entirely abolish the teaching of German. For prudential reasons they would have to keep a careful eye upon German thought and development for many a year to come.[4]

The *Western Morning News*, reporting the event, reminded its readers that German would remain the language spoken by some 80,000,000 people in Central Europe, and argued that German should be retained on commercial grounds alone. The 1918 Leathes Report[5] (*Modern Studies*) also saw problems in the public's potential willingness to accept the teaching of German in schools, but it felt strongly that precisely *because of* the War and what had led to it there should be an extension of German teaching.

By the late 1920s supporters of German on the curriculum were challenging the position of French. A Board of Education document of 1929 stated that the assumption should no longer be made that pupils' choice of foreign language should be restricted to French.[6] In 1928 there were only 3,837 School Certificate candidates in German, while French attracted 54,273 (Spanish as few as 719).

By the time of the Norwood Report (1943) the arguments were being crystallised into clear statements about the 'redressing of the balance in favour of German',[7] and the diversification debate has of course continued since then for over 45 years. From Norwood until the 1960s, when modern language teaching was injected with new enthusiasms and much rapid expansion took place, German benefited considerably from the steady decline in the teaching of Latin. In 1960 O level entries showed 135,578 candidates for French, 49,117 for Latin and 21,806 for German. Latin, then, was still in the clear position of second foreign language. However, by the summer of 1973 German entries at O level had overtaken those for Latin (German: 37,978; Latin: 36,463). In the first year of GCSE (1988) the entry figures for the main languages taught were:

Figure 1

	5th year pupils	Total entries
French	276,318	284,698
German	83,539	87,874
Spanish	12,724	13,236
Latin	8,194	8,983
Italian	976	1,590
Russian	678	1,033

While it is obvious that to be second to French in this pecking order is better than being in the position of the other languages, there are considerable disadvantages attaching to the 'second foreign language' tag. The main matter for concern is that German, as second foreign language, acquired an image (partly a result, perhaps, of its having usurped the position of Latin) of being elitist and difficult. These points were made by the Association of Teachers of German in 1978:

> The myth [that German is a difficult language] springs probably from two sources: firstly, the tendency for German to be the second foreign language taught in schools so that it is mainly the brighter children who learn it and over a shorter period of time then French. Uninformed opinion may, therefore, conclude that it is a harder language, but it could just as easily be argued that it is *easier*. Secondly there was in the past a tendency to teach German as though it were Latin, with prescribed tables of declensions for rote learning and little emphasis on learning through usage.[8]

I shall return to the questions of perceived difficulty and teaching style; first, it is necessary to consider why German should be taught in the schools of Britain.

In recent years there has been much talk of the need to promote foreign language learning in schools for trade purposes, and currently (1989) linguists are being urged to prepare for the opportunities 1992 will offer. The British Overseas Trade Board's report of 1979 put the case powerfully – and with royal imprimatur. The concluding sentence of the report summarises the reason for taking the trade question seriously:

> Now that more than 50 per cent of our trade is with countries in Western Europe and only 26 per cent of our exports go to the English speaking world . . . a knowledge of the language and culture of our overseas customers is more relevant to British export success than ever before.[9]

The Federal Republic of Germany is in fact the UK's foremost trading partner in Europe. Much has been made of a remark attributed to the former German ambassador in London to the effect that while it was possible to buy from the Germans in English, if traders wished to sell to them they would have to do so in German.

The trade link question must not be underestimated – but nor must it be given too much weight. I have argued elsewhere[10] that the degree of foreign language competence required by those playing a part in the economic role of Britain overseas is likely to be so high as to be beyond the reach of most school learners. What is vital, however, is that those with basic competencies should continue their language studies beyond an elementary level. A recent survey of the language skills of British and German Members of Parliament has shown that while only 5.8% of German *Bundestag* members claimed to speak no language other than German, 17.3% of British MPs said they had no foreign language competence. (Of the Conservative MPs taking part in the survey 66% claimed knowledge of French and 26% of German; for Labour MPs the figures were French 60%; German 32%).[11]

In the days of School Certificate the subsidiary level language examinations enabled specialists taking the Higher Certificate in other subjects to continue with their language study. Other examinations, notably a number at AO level – including 'German for Business Studies'[12] – have enabled some candidates to continue their study of German to a stage considerably higher than GCE O level or GCSE. The advent of AS level examinations will allow that trend to develop. The notion of 'languages for specific purposes' is important within the context of the encouragement of further study once a basic level has been attained, and German has a particularly good case for inclusion in school and college courses with a specific aim to develop secretarial, commercial and business competence in the language. It used to be urged that scientists needed a working knowledge of German, and while that remains desirable (it is desirable, indeed, that academics in all disciplines should have a basic reading knowledge of the language) it is now generally the case that significant papers are published in English, or at least have detailed English abstracts, and scientist colleagues tell me that English has become the language of German laboratories where their colleagues from various countries meet to work together.

How many people actually speak a given language is a factor often raised in defence of its position on the curriculum. Estimates of the number of speakers of German vary widely if not wildly. There is said to be a 'European market', to which British products might be sold, 'comprising nearly 100 million speakers of German'.[13] David Crystal[14] estimates that there are 100 million *mother tongue* speakers of German in the world (French having some 70 million, Spanish 250 million, Russian 150 million, and Italian 60 million). In Crystal's list Spanish ranks third, Russian seventh, German tenth, French eleventh and Italian fifteenth in the pecking order. A German government report on the position of German in the world[15] estimates some 40 million German speakers worldwide (excluding those in the Federal and German Democratic Republics). An ATG/Goethe-Institut pamphlet reports 120 million mother tongue speakers. Clearly the estimated number of German speakers is large enough for German to be taken seriously as a language of significant importance in the world.

There is too another supporting argument. If German is not a 'world language' in the sense that English is, it is what Stuart Parkes[16] has called a 'worlds language' inasmuch as it is still to a significant extent the *lingua franca* of many countries in Eastern Europe and therefore *the* language common to both East and West. The German government report of 1985 estimates some one million German speakers in Poland, 350,000 in Romania, two million in Czechoslovakia, 1,200,000 in Hungary and several million in the USSR.[17] Visitors to Hungary and Czechoslovakia find German especially helpful; restaurant menus, for example, in Budapest and Prague will often be bilingual, and there will not always be English versions available.

It is necessary to consider in some detail the question of how difficult a language German is. Language difficulty is a slippery concept (Hawkins has much of interest to say on the subject[18]), and what points can be made inevitably centre on subjective views and speculation:

> While it must be logically true that an average native English speaker will find language X easier to learn than language Y and language Y easier than language Z, it would be very difficult, if not impossible, to demonstrate objectively that that is in fact the case.[19]

Anne Keene concludes in her examination of the perceived difficulties of German that the language is closer to English in the early stages of learning than French:

> The regular sound system and its consistent correlation with the spelling, the logical grammar . . . and the vocabulary with its similarities to English suggest German as a logical choice of foreign language for English speakers.[20]

Certainly the cognates help considerably in the early lessons, and there is a view shared by many that listening (and understanding) in German is more straightforward for the average (and lower ability) English pupil than in the Romance languages. Margaret Tumber believes that:

> German, when spoken even moderately carefully by native speakers is rarely a complete jumble of sound. Presented with the aim of developing listening skills in the classroom German can not only increase the confidence of language learners but also make a positive contribution to the development of a skill . . . neglected in other subject areas.[21]

Tumber's view is supported in part by the findings of the largest investigation so far undertaken of pupil performance in French, German and Spanish, the Assessment of Performance Unit's (APU) survey, undertaken in 1983:

> The pattern in German, of higher scores in listening than in reading, contrasts with results in French and Spanish [. . .] The strong suggestion that English speaking pupils find the phonological system in German more accessible, because there are more recognisable and consistent associations with the written language, is supported by the finding that German listening was one of the only two areas in which the performance of pupils whose first language was not English was significantly lower than that of English speaking pupils.[22]

Josefina Bello[23] is harsher on German than Keene (1984), particularly in her analysis of grammatical complexity: the case system which results in complications for the quick assimilation of forms of the definite article, the possessive adjective, etc. But on balance the direct 'accessibility' of German in the early stages of learning has long been recognised as a strong argument in favour of the language. Here is a view of over 65 years ago:

> . . . many school pupils, who have struggled for years to get their tongues adapted to the French vocables, have acquired the rudiments of German with comparative ease.[24]

And in a survey of opinion among some 250 fifth and seventh year pupils Phillips and Stencel found that those pupils finding German grammar easier than French most commonly described German grammar as 'more consistent', 'more logical', 'more straightforward' or 'more clear-cut'.[25]

Questions of perceived difficulty cannot of course be divorced from the learning situation. Phillips and Stencel found in their survey that of all the reasons quoted for one language being found easier than another, 58% related to factors other than the language itself. Pupils who found French easier, for example, said that that was because they had been learning the language for longer. Others quoted previous visits abroad as an important factor in their present perception of difficulty as between two or more languages, and, as must be expected, teaching method and the teacher him- or herself were seen as major contributing factors.[26]

As we have seen, German has often suffered on the curriculum of British schools by being consistently in the position of *second* foreign language, taught mainly to abler pupils over a shorter course (of two, three, or four years, the national preference being for three years, i.e. a third-year start), and by being taught often as an alternative to or replacement for, Latin, inheriting some of the teaching approaches used for that language.

In German, as in other languages (not least Spanish and Italian) there have been courses, like *Aufenthalt in Deutschland* (1949), or *Deutsches Leben* (1931) or Greatwood's *School German Course* (1958), whose style is rooted in the classical tradition. Such courses prepared generations of pupils thoroughly – and appropriately – for School Certificate and O level examinations which relied heavily on accurate translation from and into the (literary) language. They were followed over many years by various 'compromise' courses, like Rowlinson's *Sprich mal Deutsch* (1967) and Shotter's *Deutscher Sprachkurs* (1973), alongside courses based in developing audio-lingual and audio-visual methodology such as Paxton and Brake's *Wir Lernen Deutsch* (1970) and the seminal Nuffield/Schools Council course *Vorwärts* (1968),[27] the precursor of many of today's 'communicative' courses.

Given the fact that before the publication of *Vorwärts* and its successors most coursebooks were 'traditional' in style, and given the composition of German classes in most schools and the fact that courses to public examination level were usually only of three years duration, it is scarcely surprising that many teachers of German have in the past preferred to use what Ann Miller has referred to as a 'grammatical/analytical/academic/formal/structural'[28] approach. That teachers tended to opt for styles subsumed under that all-embracing description was clear from a 1979 survey Miller conducted of teacher opinion in Oxfordshire, and this was borne out by a later study[29] in which it was shown that in a sample of 66 teachers (mainly teachers of German) there was a clear preference for 'a more formal grammatical approach' when teaching shorter second foreign language courses to selected or self-selecting pupils. Of the teachers of German (53 in all) over 75% felt that such an approach was necessary and/or desirable.

But since that research was undertaken, and since coursebooks of the kind I have mentioned have been written, many important advances in modern language teaching and in policy provision have taken place, among them the graded objectives movement, the development of 'communicative' approaches to modern language teaching (inherited from EFL teaching), and the advent of GCSE.

Communicative styles of teaching have resulted in a new generation of coursebooks, led by the phenomenally popular *Deutsch Heute*, which have built on the new approaches. Many of the new courses have a freshness and vitality, and an authenticity, that most of their predecessors lacked. It is in fact the peculiarly British problem that the language of modern language coursebooks (and particularly, it seems, those in German) is often artificial and unnatural in a sense that coursebooks written abroad would not be. Jochen Kapuste takes many an author to task in a perceptive article on language and reality in English-produced German coursebooks:

> ... *in diesem Punkt, Authentizität, hält kein Lehrbuch, das älter als 5 Jahre ist, dem Anspruch stand, die von deutschen Sprechern gebrauchte Sprache einigermaßen adäquat zu vermitteln.*[30]

He quotes examples of wrong usage (*studieren* in school contexts, for example) and of what he calls '*Englisch mit deutschen Wörtern*'. Where more recent texts meet with his approval he is still able to demonstrate – convincingly – that they could be made better. For:

> *Was machen wir heute abend?*
> *Möchtest du ins Kino gehen?*

he suggests:

> *Du, was machen wir denn heute abend?*
> *Heute abend? Ich weiß nicht. Wir können ja ins Kino gehen.*[31]

which makes the exchange natural and has an authentic 'feel' about it that is often lacking. A quick glance at, say, German coursebooks produced for school learners in Sweden or in Hungary will show clearly that the kind of language used is qualitatively quite different from that found in books produced in Britain. Perhaps authors should collaborate far more with German colleagues.

Kapuste mentions the effective use of juvenile literature in language teaching in Holland – there is available to British teachers of German the excellent *Scala Jugendmagazin* produced by Inter-Nationes in Bonn-Bad Godesberg – and he laments the fact that pupils are given few opportunities to show emotion and to use their imagination in the coursebooks he has examined. Many activities associated with communicative approaches to language teaching do in fact allow pupils to engage with the language in the way that Kapuste would like to see. Pair-work exercises, for example, if properly conducted, provide a lot of scope in the right direction.

Rosemary Davidson[32] estimates that German publications constitute some 23% of the total of modern language titles produced by ten main British publishers with German books on their lists. This is a generously high proportion, considering the ratio of learners of German to learners of French.

She attributes the large number of books produced to the fact that most modern languages editors in publishing houses tend to be graduates in two languages, and to a 'a feeling of responsibility amongst publishers for the well-being of German as a subject'. With this goodwill, and with the production of a range of new coursebooks in recent years, together with a wealth of skills-based support materials, the teacher of German now has no shortage of excellent – and for the most part purpose-built – teaching materials.

The BBC and Thames Television have continued too to produce audio and visual material of high quality. The latter's series *Partner* in particular has been found to be very successful and flexible in classroom use. At the same time the Goethe-Institut provides German teachers with a remarkable range of support; Inter-Nationes sends to any German teacher requesting them, free copies of highly professionally produced teaching materials for all levels.

There are, then, materials in great profusion for German teaching at all levels. Since the language has traditionally been taught over a shorter period than French, there is, however, still a lack of five-book courses which allow a first-year start, and many existing three-book courses have difficulty in pitching the material in the first book at an appropriate level (is it aimed at 11 year olds learning German as a first foreign language, or at 12, 13 or 14 year olds learning German as a second foreign language?). With the development of diversification policies publishers will no doubt be bending their minds to the production of coursebooks which assume five years of study.

In considering what the future holds for German in schools, it is possible to be optimistic. I would suggest six reasons for an optimistic outlook, each of which will have to be tempered by a caveat.

(1)   There is at last a proper policy of diversification of provision for first foreign language teaching. The dominance of French on the secondary school curriculum is beginning to diminish, and there is now a real chance for the rapid expansion (already seen in a number of LEAs) of five-year courses in German. (The latest figures indicate that some 8% of secondary schools offer German as first or alternative first foreign language[33]).

(2)   Approaches to modern language teaching have made enormous strides forward in recent years, and there is every reason to suppose that German will continue to benefit from communicative teaching in its present manifestation.

(3)   Syllabuses in schools – themselves conditioned as ever by the demands of public examinations – have changed remarkably, if not as dramatically as many would have liked, so that children are beginning to be able to demonstrate what they can do, instead of what they do not know. GCSE must be reckoned an enormous leap forward in this respect, and already in German it is possible to feel satisfied at the increased proportion, compared with O level, of children gaining A grades.

(4) The National Curriculum, as enshrined in the 1988 Education Reform Act, will require all children to study a foreign language throughout the five years of compulsory secondary education. Despite the fears that the anticipation of such an expansion of foreign language teaching brings, the very fact that pupils will no longer be able to drop their language studies at the earliest opportunity is bound to solve one problem and contribute greatly to solving another. The first is the gender bias: modern linguists at most levels are predominantly female – in the 11 to 16 age group there will eventually be parity between boys and girls, as is the case in schools on the continent. German classes will no longer have the gender imbalance inevitable when selection for second foreign language study depends on results in first year French examinations. The second is the question of motivation: there is some evidence from existing good practice to suggest that where children do *not* have the opportunity to abandon their language study at 14 they are better motivated.[34]

(5) Resources of all kinds for the teaching of German are excellent, as indicated above.

(6) There are signs at last that there is no longer a need to keep making a case for the learning of German as opposed to French. The climate is good for the introduction of German where it has not been taught before, and every opportunity should now be seized to make sure that that happens.

For each of these reasons for optimism, however, caveats must be entered:

(1) Diversification depends on adequate staffing, and there are few signs to indicate that the future supply of German teachers will be adequate to facilitate the expansion that Germanists would like to see.

(2) Though communicative language teaching has much to offer that is good, even exciting, I do not consider it to be a *method* in the sense, for example, that audio-visual teaching was: if it turns into dogma in the way that so many methods of the past did, it will serve the cause of language teaching very ill indeed. There must be scope – and particularly in the teaching of a language like German which cannot ignore some formal teaching of grammar and syntax, for what I have called 'a new eclecticism' in language teaching, which draws on the strengths of *all* approaches (and I mean *all* – even the discredited grammar-translation method has techniques to offer, and no teacher should feel guilty or ashamed at using techniques which do not accord with orthodox opinion).

(3) Despite advances in coursebook writing and in syllabus design, there is some way to go before we can be fully satisfied. There is still too much English used in published materials, and GCSE syllabuses still contain some dubious exercises left over from earlier eras; in addition they do not at present contain a course-work element, and have scarcely profited from the widely accepted principles of the Graded Objectives Movement.

(4) The provisions of the National Curriculum will result in considerable expansion of German as first foreign language, but this will be balanced by a reduction in second foreign language teaching, since the expectation is that schools will start the second foreign language in Year 4. It is extraordinary that it can be argued that all the excellent features of GCSE, which will take a long time to realise and which depend on careful and time-consuming communicative styles of teaching, are worthwhile, while at the same time the second foreign language is relegated to just over five terms of study to examination level. The effects on teaching methods will be disastrous, and in German we are bound to see recourse to the 'grammatical/analytical/academic/formal/structural' style of the past.

(5) Though resources are generally very good, they are best used precisely as *resources*: all coursebooks (and those in German are no exception) stifle teaching initiative if followed slavishly: an eclectic teaching style avoids the problems.

(6) Though the case for German is now made, it will be a mistake to be complacent. Future development will have to be closely monitored in case difficulties of staffing (in particular) cause a slide back to the present severe imbalance of provision.

'I heard a Californian student in Heidelberg say, in one of his calmest moods', says Mark Twain (in *A Tramp Abroad*), 'that he would rather decline two drinks than one German adjective'. *'Aber potztausend Donnerwetter!'* wrote a mid-nineteenth-century Professor of Modern Languages and Literature at Harvard,

> What a language it is to be sure! With ... sentences in which one sets sail like an admiral with sealed orders, not knowing where the devil he is going till he is in midocean! [...] The confounded genders! If I die I will have engraved on my tombstone that I died of *der, die, das*, not because I caught 'em, but because I couldn't.[35]

Even Schulz's Snoopy has had difficulties:

> Here's the World War I Flying Ace Studying his German Phrase Book ... *Ich, meiner, mir, mich; du, deiner, dir, dich; der, dessen, dem, den, die, deren, der, die; aus, außer, bei, mit, nach, seit, von, zu ... an, auf, hinter, in, neben, über, unter* – I SURRENDER!![36]

As we have seen, German teaching is not, and need not be, as daunting as that. *Deutsche Sprache, schwere Sprache* is a catchphrase that should begin now to lose its meaning in the German classroom of the future.

Italian in School, College and University

Bob Powell

Ten years ago

In July 1979, 50 or so Italian enthusiasts met together for three days at the University of York to take part in a colloquium on the teaching of Italian in the UK.[1] Most sectors of the educational world were represented. Participants listened to practising teachers working in schools where Italian was offered as first foreign language and to teachers designing graded tests and other kinds of examinations in Italian. Also present were lecturers from polytechnics and universities who spoke encouragingly of current intake levels and future degree course plans. Initial teacher education and in-service prospects were also surveyed. There was a strong presence from the Italian Education Inspectorate and Italian Government funded teachers who provided *corsi integrativi* (supplementary courses) for the children of the Italian community in Britain.

Despite the evident enthusiasm, conviction and enterprise of those present, the image of Italian that emerged during the colloquium was that of a language struggling to survive in the school curriculum and liable to be subjected to increasing pressure during the years to come. Successful experiences were identified and publicised but these tended to be rare, isolated examples. Provision at all levels was patchy, dependent more on the goodwill of committed individuals than a coherently worked-out policy. Even the most optimistic assessment of the future prospects for Italian were tinged with doubt. Generally the tenor of the contributions was sober and realistic. It was understood that the anticipated diminishing resources and falling rolls of the 1980s posed a real threat.

As one of the participants in that colloquium, I find it quite a challenge one decade later to analyse the state of health of the language I love. How has Italian fared in the 1980s? Has there been the hoped-for expansion? Or will a review of school examination entries and uptake at higher education level indicate a decline in provision? Might the fate of this minority language be irrevocably sealed, notwithstanding all the encouraging talk of diversification, by the implementation of the National Curriculum? These are some of the questions which I hope to answer in this contribution. I shall also attempt to provide counter-arguments to the reasons so often cited for *not* including Italian in the school curriculum. There are perfectly understandable reasons reflecting anxieties over teacher supply. There are, however, others more symptomatic of a resistance to change and an unwillingness on the part of curriculum planners, at departmental and whole school level, to experiment with alternative patterns of foreign language provision and assessment.

Examination courses

In terms of the outcomes of curricular provision, as measured by the numbers of candidates taking public examinations in a given subject, Italian and Russian have always lagged behind German and Spanish, the other 'second languages' usually on offer. I do not propose to produce masses of statistics illustrating the ranking order of languages in this respect or to chart the fluctuating patterns of entries and passes over the years. However, it is clear that there has been, unfortunately, a marked decline in the status of Italian in schools.

Between 1975 and 1985, there was a 44.7% drop in the numbers of pupils entered for GCE Ordinary level in England and Wales. At Advanced level, the drop was 18.1%. It must be remembered that this decade was one in which the population curve for 16 year olds peaked at about 841,000 in 1981.[2] The only areas of growth as far as Italian was concerned were in the CSE examinations in England and Wales (a 39% increase in entries) and in Northern Ireland. In the latter, the numbers involved are very small indeed. Figure 1 provides more details.

Figure 1

School examination entries in Italian

	England and Wales			N. Ireland		Scotland	
	CSE	*GCE O*	*GCE A*	*GCE O*	*GCE A*	*O Grade*	*A Grade*
1975	472	4456	833	60	20	495	248
1985	656	2464	682	138	35	320	185
% change	+39.0	−44.7	−18.1	+130	+175	−35.4	−25.8

Source: Centre for Information on Language Teaching and Research

Two points are worthy of note following closer scrutiny of Italian examination entries. Firstly, the sex imbalance – girls outnumber boys by as much as four to one. This is an aspect of Italian teaching that had already caught my attention several years ago.[3] Secondly, if one deducts from the totals those candidates entered by independent schools, the numbers dwindle to the equivalent of a handful of classes. The image of Italian – and the reality of Italian teaching for the majority of learners – emerges as that of a language primarily confined to girls in private schools. It remains to be seen whether the GCSE examination will be considered more accessible to pupils in comprehensive schools. Certainly the emphasis on communicative skills should, in theory, make a second foreign language course less of a daunting prospect. However, any advantage gained by the more practical focus of the assessment procedures seems to be erased by the proposition that beginners' courses in a second foreign language will begin later than previously thought desirable, i.e. in Years 4 and 5. Even here there is little curriculum time available once the National Curriculum's core and foundation subjects have been allotted their spaces on the timetable.

Other courses in school

Besides the more conventional examination classes, Italian can be found in a variety of forms in schools. I recently conducted an informal survey of former students of mine who were keen to teach Italian in the schools to which they had been appointed. It revealed that Italian was being taught in a number of different contexts. In some cases the new teachers had designed compact courses which were being offered usually on an elective basis, for example, as a part of a sixth-form general studies programme. In other cases, the languages department, having decided to offer a range of languages in the lower school as part of a series of taster courses, was pleased to welcome the opportunity to include Italian in the menu. In a couple of schools Italian was being offered to lower ability children in the second or third years as part of a 'fresh start' policy. It was reported to me by one teacher that, although she had found initially that the atmosphere in her bottom set Year 3 class had been, in her understated terms, 'not the most conducive for continuing foreign language learning', the children had fairly rapidly warmed to Italian, finding it an easier language to pronounce and remember than the French they had abandoned. Pupils were encouraged to take graded tests at various levels in Italian.

Italian can also play an important role in fostering multicultural understanding, for example, as a component of language awareness courses. In schools attended by pupils from an Italian background such initiatives can provide bilingual pupils with a welcome opportunity to display their linguistic skills.

It is impossible to monitor the extent to which courses such as the above operate in schools in the UK. Numerous attempts have been made over the past few years to produce an accurate list of schools where Italian was being taught. The Association of Teachers of Italian (ATI) has attempted to keep records, through its membership lists, of schools and colleges offering Italian. But there are enormous problems in keeping such records up to date. Although during the academic year 1988 to 1989 there were nearly 600 members, not all Italian teachers elect to join their specialist subject professional association. Also, Italian is one of those minority subjects which can slip in and out of the school curriculum from year to year. Even members of Her Majesty's Inspectorate who have demonstrated their support for Italian by directing short in-service courses and obtaining funding for intensive language courses in Italy have found it well nigh impossible to state with authority how much Italian is being taught in British schools in any one year, and exactly where Italian classes may be found – to be inspected!

Notwithstanding the view expressed in the first national statement of policy on modern languages by the Secretaries of State for Education that 'in trading terms alone . . . there is . . . a strong need for Italian . . .',[4] the position of this language in British schools, it must be acknowledged, is precarious. Indeed, the fine words in the policy statement exhorting LEAs to increase the range of languages in their schools will seem worthless in ten years' time if the long awaited expansion in provision does not take place.

There are, however, some grounds for optimism. There are a number of useful diversification projects taking place across the country. The 'Diversification of First Foreign Language' pilot project initiated by Government and funded by means of an Education Support Grant (ESG) is being carried out in ten LEAs. Not unexpectedly, Italian does not have a major role in the implementation and evaluation of the programmes. It features in only three of the LEAs, only in one school having been adopted as first foreign language. Yet, in a number of other locations the project may have provided the necessary impetus for schools to develop Italian as a second choice following the core language provision. The Oxford Project on Diversification of First Foreign Language Teaching (OXPROD), in its study of pupil attitudes, progress and organisational aspects, has included one school where Italian is taught as one of a range of first foreign languages. It is important, if Italian is not to be further marginalised, that it features in experiments of this kind.

The outcomes of these investigations remain to be seen. Undoubtedly they will provide much needed information about the practicalities involved in offering greater choice to parents and pupils. Already the idea that diversification can take place only in large schools is being challenged. The evaluation reports may also provide some concrete evidence that children respond positively and make excellent progress when given the chance to learn Italian. This may encourage other schools to introduce Italian or extend contact time for the subject.

Italian mother tongue teaching

Since 1971 the Italian government has sponsored the teaching of Italian to the children of Italian origin in British schools. Teachers are appointed by the Ministry of Education in Rome and paid directly through the Italian Consulate in this country. At the time of the *Italian in Schools Colloquium* in 1979 it was reported that there were about 12,000 children in the United Kingdom attending nearly 800 classes of this type.[5] Over 150 peripatetic teachers were employed 'from Portsmouth to Inverness' to carry out the teaching.

Originally these classes were set up with the expressed aim of facilitating the return to Italy of the children of Italian emigrants.[6] The notion of return has always tended to linger in Italian immigrants' minds. During the 1970s and 1980s it is estimated that many families returned to Italy. Today, therefore, the numbers involved reflect the needs of a smaller Italian community. There are now 112 teachers servicing about 700 classes involving about 8,000 pupils.[7]

Classes are held either after school hours (*doposcuola*) or within the school day (*corsi inseriti*). In the latter case, pupils are withdrawn from other lessons. In evidence to the Committee of Enquiry into the Education of Ethnic Minority Children several of the teachers lamented the fact that their classes were seen by some pupils as an imposition, especially if they were held after the school day.[8] Where English mother tongue speakers were also allowed to attend, the lessons seemed to gain in status both with the children for whom they were originally intended and as an element of the school's foreign language provision.

Much as one can admire the Italian Government's initiative in setting up the scheme and its continuing support through the years, it is my belief that the *corsi integrativi* did little originally to further the cause of Italian as part of mainstream foreign language provision in this country. On the contrary, I fear that the availability of these courses added to the general impression that Italian was, literally, a minority language best suited to the children of Italian families and not really eligible as a realistic alternative to French or German. Similar concern was expressed during submissions to the Committee of Enquiry, as well as questions about the nature and quality of the teaching carried out largely by untrained persons or persons trained for an Italian education system.

More recently, however, it appears that at least one recommendation of the Committee of Enquiry has been heeded. In a few schools the *corsi integrativi* have been timetabled into the whole school curriculum, thereby giving all pupils the opportunity to learn Italian. It has certainly been the aim of those responsible for this teaching in Britain since 1986 that wherever possible the classes should be open to all pupils in the schools in which they take place. Since the second Italian national conference on emigration in November 1988, support for this policy has been official. It may have created a greater pedagogical challenge for the teachers who will have to cope with a wider range of pupil ability and experience, but it should serve to increase the numbers of pupils who consider Italian as a serious option. In some schools the teaching has extended into A level work. If this pattern of provision extends to all the schools in the scheme the prospects for Italian will be much improved.

Italian in further and adult education

It is generally assumed that there is more Italian taught in the further education and adult education sectors than in secondary schools. I certainly subscribe to that view, but it is extremely difficult to provide evidence to support the theory. There are no centrally collected data which would enable the researcher to provide an accurate picture of provision. It is easy to anticipate the problems that would be encountered by anyone wishing to fill this statistical gap. Many of the non-vocational courses offered by FE colleges last less than a year. Some of the *ab initio* courses for holiday-makers and business people may last ten weeks or even less. Continuity of courses from year to year usually depends solely on the principle of supply and demand. And there are strict regulations regarding the viability of courses relating to the volume of the enrolment and, hence, class size. The teaching staff engaged in this work are, in most cases, part-time tutors who will not feature on the establishments' permanent staff list.

Some years ago, a survey conducted by the Language Centre at Brighton Polytechnic[9] provided some indication of the popularity of foreign language learning among adults. Information was gathered from 380 centres, that is from approximately 65% of the total in England and Wales. Between them they offered 4,719 classes in modern languages which were attended by 64,529 adults. In the autumn term of 1983, 5,182 mature students had embarked on courses in Italian in these centres, at beginners', second stage or advanced levels. Judging by enrolment figures in local colleges this interest has not waned. Similarly, if sales of BBC course textbooks are anything to go by, there is considerable interest in the Italian language among the adult population.[10]

The majority of FE colleges also offer vocational courses and non-vocational courses leading to an examination. Besides the usual courses to GCSE and A level, there may be programmes of work towards certificates awarded by the Royal Society of Arts (RSA) or the Institute of Linguists (IOL), to name just two of the several organisations concerned with 'alternative' forms of foreign language testing. Over the past few years interest in Italian has remained steady. Institute of Linguist examination entries have, in fact, increased gradually each year, with now over 500 people taking tests at various levels.

The worth of these examinations and the opportunities for working in Italian in the international trade world have yet to be fully appreciated by teachers, parents, students and employers. There are, however, encouraging signs that business and commercial firms are at last beginning to recognise the need for negotiators fluent in other languages and for other members of personnel involved in public relations to have at least some confidence in communicating in another language. Italy, it should be remembered, is one of our major trading partners.

Italian in higher education

Italian as main subject of an undergraduate course of study is offered currently in 26 universities and polytechnics in the United Kingdom. Ten years ago the total was 35. In all but three of the institutions provision is made for the student wishing to study the language *ab initio*. Italian is usually taken to degree level jointly with another subject. Most frequently this is another foreign language, but in recent years the choice has increased dramatically. There are now no fewer than 287 combined degree programmes in which Italian features.[11]

Academics in Italian departments, in order to survive in a world that demands greater vocational relevance, have responded ingeniously to the changing climate, even if some of them retain what is predominantly an academic, humanistic view of language teaching and learning.[12] Some smaller departments were closed in the early eighties during rationalisation programmes implemented by the University Grants Committee (UGC). However the 'health' of the language in higher education appears reasonably sound, despite these closures, with enrolments steady or increasing in a number of departments.[13]

It is estimated that approximately 300 people graduate each year with Italian as principal subject or joint subject of their degree. Without a direct survey of Italian departments, it is impossible to be more accurate. The official DES statistics provide details for French, German and Spanish, but Italian graduates are included under the heading 'Other European Languages'. This is an unfortunate gap in the information available, in terms of teaching potential, and it makes realistic forecasting extremely difficult.

Italian in initial teacher education

In the academic year 1988 to 1989, there were 10,136 students following the Postgraduate Certificate in Education (PGCE) courses in a wide range of subjects. Of these, 879 were foreign linguists, 676 of whom were on courses in University Departments of Education (UDEs); the remaining 203 were in Polytechnics or Colleges of Higher Education. By a remarkable coincidence there were 676 women and 203 men on these courses but they were not, of course, segregated by sex, nor by institution![14]

The precise number of graduates in any one year who have the potential to offer Italian as a teaching subject is open to speculation. The figures collected by the Graduate Teacher Training Registry (GTTR), the clearing house for applications, provide evidence of the main language by which the courses are designated. They also show the subsidiary subject where there are separate courses offered by institutions. However, there is only a handful of training courses where Italian is named as a component of the PGCE programme. There may be other minor course elements but, falling short of the officially recognised length for subsidiary courses, they may not be formally identified.

In 1988 to 1989 there were only a dozen or so students in the system who were identified as having Italian as main subject. This small number would hardly make much of an impression on the staffing in schools. Yet many more student teachers may have the linguistic and practical skills needed to increase provision for Italian. They are not identified by current statistical procedures.

In 1979, in a national survey of PGCE courses, I discovered that there were 64 such teachers.[15] The Department of Education and Science during 1988 surveyed teacher training institutions in order to find out what expertise they might be able to offer in modern languages other than French and to enquire about the potential for in-service training in order to upgrade 'rusty language skills for serving teachers'. Questions were also asked about the pattern of student entry over recent years and the languages they could offer to future employers. The questionnaire results may not have revealed the presence of scores of future teachers ready immediately to involve themselves fully in the teaching of Italian. But they will surely have shown that there are many language graduates who, with further professional development, would be able to make a valuable contribution to the expansion of Italian provision.

It is, of course, unwise to rely solely on the influx of newly qualified teachers to boost provision for Italian. There is, nonetheless, potential for growth in initial teacher education. The diversification process currently taking place in schools needs to be initiated, at a national level, within teacher education. A number of institutions could be identified as having a particular language role and, with proper financial support, the training of future teachers of Italian could be more secure than hitherto. It would also greatly assist schools considering introducing Italian, or simply wishing to maintain provision, if they could locate more easily the language specialists required. LEAs and schools using the 'licensed teacher' route for recruitment would also benefit from knowing where they could find support for the training and induction of Italian licensees. After 1992, and with teacher training qualifications of the different member states being recognised across the European Community, there are likely to be more Italian nationals seeking employment in this country. There is currently a surplus of teachers of English in Italy.

Teachers in service

According to the figures presented as an annex to the DES *Statement of Policy*[16], there were (in 1984) 130 teachers in post with Italian as the main subject of their highest qualification, usually a Bachelor's degree. Only 50 were teaching Italian. There were a further 1,520 teachers with some qualification in Italian but only twenty of these were engaged in teaching the language. There is clearly, in management terms, some slack in the system. Many teachers would welcome the chance to teach Italian but they are currently employed as teachers of another language, usually French.

Four reasons for not including Italian in the school curriculum

During my visits to schools to supervise students on teaching practice, whenever possible I ask senior members of staff whether they have ever considered, or would consider in the future, introducing Italian into the curriculum in some form or other. I have asked these questions especially in schools where I have known there to be somebody in the language department capable of teaching the subject. Inevitably, I receive mostly negative responses, sympathetic in tone maybe ('Of course we'd like to expand our language teaching . . .'), but negative all the same.

Many of the reasons against including Italian in the secondary school curriculum can be anticipated from my review of the current state of Italian teaching in the preceding paragraphs. Some of the arguments, it must be admitted, appear overwhelming. Nevertheless, the case for Italian needs constantly to be reaffirmed. Recommendations for improving the situation can also be offered in a discussion of the future prospects for the language.

Reason 1: 'There's no demand for it.'
It may be true that parents and pupils are not clamouring at the doors of schools protesting about the absence of Italian. However, it is generally the case that very little by way of consumer surveys is conducted by curriculum designers in schools to ascertain the preferences of the public. Consultation with parents over the contents of the curriculum is becoming not just more fashionable, but a prerequisite for curriculum change. Italian is in demand in other sectors of education, notably in institutions of further and higher education. In an increasingly competitive world, where schools are vying with each other for new pupils, it is the school that offers something a little different that may attract parents.

Reason 2: 'We couldn't staff it anyway.'
It is my experience that in many language departments there are people who would welcome the opportunity to teach Italian. While recognising that continuity of staffing is a real problem in any shortage subject, the problem for Italian may not be totally insurmountable. Schools that opt for languages other than French tend to attract applicants for vacant posts precisely because these teachers wish to teach their specialist language. What is needed is better communication between the trainers, LEAs and schools. A national register, possibly held by CILT, should be set up and properly funded. Certain training institutions should be given additional resourcing to increase their 'output' in Italian and other less commonly taught languages. Larger numbers of graduates with Italian as part of their degree would be attracted into teaching if they knew that they could have appropriate specialist training and enhanced opportunities for teaching their chosen subject later.

Reason 3: 'Italian is not an important language to learn.'
I have never found arguments about the relative importance of foreign languages very convincing. They generally stem from an excessively narrow-minded opinion about the cultural status of a language or from inaccurate knowledge about volumes of international trade. If these economic justifications had been converted into curriculum priorities, German would surely have been the first foreign language in British schools for the past twenty years. Instead, we have been bound by a model of the curriculum, founded on a nineteenth-century philosophy, more connected with diplomatic desirability than with economic realities. It is becoming a cliché to talk of the possibilities of the free European market of the 1990s, and the cynics may say they have heard it all before as Britain prepared to join the EEC. Yet 1992 represents a fundamentally different and greater opportunity. The call for more varied foreign language provision in schools should be heeded. Italian should be given equal status as we prepare for the European free market.

Reason 4: 'Most of our children go to France or Spain, if they go abroad on holiday.'

It is undoubtedly true that France and Spain are the most popular destinations for British holidaymakers. Yet increasing numbers of families are finding Italy an attractive place to spend the summer break. However, justifying a curriculum subject by linking its content to possible holiday activities is a pretty unsound way to plan children's education, even when it is a question of foreign language choice. Educational reasons for learning foreign languages must take precedence. The reasons for Italian being the target for foreign language learning are as valid as they are for French. It is my experience that some children find the language less daunting than other European languages. Moreover, Italian, to a greater degree than French or German, is one of Britain's community languages. Opportunities for direct communication with members of the Italian community exist in many areas of the country, and there are scores of Italian schools queueing up to link with British schools.

Conclusion

The power of individual teachers to bring about change in the whole curriculum is limited; the power of individual initial trainers to effect changes in teacher supply is virtually non-existent. In the former the way forward must be through a departmental campaign which involves not just the senior management of the school but parents, governors, local advisers and the community around the school. In the latter, the approach must be through contacts with those who determine target numbers nationally and who allocate the associated levels of funding.

Ten years ago there was little talk of diversification. There was no national policy which made this concept one of its prime goals. Today, however, there is a much more clearly defined framework for expansion. With more precise surveys being conducted at national and local level to ascertain the shortfall in linguistic expertise and the potential for expansion, there are signs that the policy makers are, at last, really serious about improving the nation's foreign language education.

I believe that there are many people who would like to see Italian included in the development and implementation of policies for diversification of foreign languages in British schools. It is, perhaps, regrettable that the responsibility for promoting Italian teaching and learning rests, as it did ten years ago, in the hands of a few committed individuals. They now need to state their case even more vigorously. They need to take a more active role in promoting the language within their particular sphere of influence. They must ensure that Italian features in every document about foreign language provision, teacher supply and training, in every piece of research about diversification and in every conversation about the national curriculum and languages in school.

─────────────── 4 ───────────────

Russian Renaissance?

David Rix and Robert Pullin

Things are looking up again for Russian, and there are encouraging indications of positive initiatives around the country. Russian looks all set to boom in Birmingham and Barnsley. At Firth Park School in Sheffield 240 young learners are having a taste of Russian in Year 1, with many choosing to learn it in Year 2. In the success story of Russian teaching at Wolverhampton High School for Girls, Russian is taught from age 11, and there are now over 200 pupils in the school taking Russian out of a total roll of approximately 550. There are also reports of a significant expansion in the numbers of pupils learning Russian as a second foreign language, for example, in Essex and Croydon. In Scotland, the Strathclyde Region has initiated a policy of diversification, and Fortrose Academy has introduced Russian as a second foreign language in Year 3. Nottinghamshire has run refresher courses for 'unused' teachers of Russian to meet new needs of teacher supply.

Demand for Russian is on the increase, and the DES policy of diversification now presents a golden opportunity for the consolidation and extension of Russian teaching in schools, whether as an alternative first or second foreign language. Conditions are favourable, and the time has come for Russian to take its place in schools and be taught as a modern language on an equal footing alongside French, German, Italian and Spanish. The opportunity is there. Shall we succeed, the second time around?

Past experience

For many years Russian teaching has struggled to reach a viable, stable position in the school curriculum. To look back briefly at the past, we all remember the exciting period of innovation and rapid expansion of Russian in the early 1960s, the time of sputniks, Gagarin's first flight in space, and the Annan Report (1962)[1] which called for the teaching of Russian to be brought up to a level of parity with German as a matter of national urgency.

We remember too the Primary French pilot scheme, and the hope expressed in Schools Council Working Paper No. 8 (1966) that 'the claims of German, Russian and Spanish would be met to a considerable extent by the increased opportunities for the learning of a second modern language at the secondary stage which the experiment, if successful, would open up'.[2] New teaching methods were introduced, and the Nuffield audio-visual courses, *Vorwärts!*, *Vperyod!* and *Adelante!* were designed to stimulate the teaching of German, Russian and Spanish to younger learners.

However, this first attempt to encourage wider teaching of languages other than French in the early years of secondary school did not come to fruition. Primary school French had the opposite effect to that expected, and in any event was discontinued. The reorganisation of secondary schools on comprehensive lines posed practical problems for language teaching. The new need to teach a modern language across the ability range produced particular methodological problems. The net result was that French became even more firmly entrenched in the first year of secondary school.

This period of 'euphoria and disenchantment' has been charted in detail by Hawkins,[3] and more recently related to the present context of diversification by Phillips.[4] Russian, in particular, suffered badly in this period of dashing of hopes, and through the 1970s and early 1980s there was a gradual but steady decline in the number of state schools in which Russian was taught. (It should be noted that Russian remained strong in independent schools, where it continues to thrive and flourish.)

It is a tribute to the enthusiasm and tenacity of teachers of Russian that the language has survived in schools. But in those schools where it has survived (on past surveys estimated at roughly 400 schools), it is still very much alive and kicking. Moreover, teachers of Russian have not only managed to cling on, but also to succeed in adapting to new teaching methods, producing new teaching materials, and promoting wider educational contacts with the Soviet Union. The time has come for them to reap the rewards for their efforts.

A fresh opportunity

Now, in 1989, there is a renewed spirit of optimism prevalent in the world of Russian teaching. A whole series of positive developments have come together at the same time, and prospects for the consolidation and extension of Russian teaching in schools are better today than they have ever been.

The climate is favourable. On the international scene relations with the USSR have improved dramatically. Cultural and educational contacts have increased. On the economic front there are greatly enhanced trade prospects.

Within the USSR the long period of stagnation has been superseded by the Gorbachev era of *perestroika* and *glasnost,* and this has kindled a strong resurgence of Western interest in the Soviet Union.

Reforms in the USSR have coincided with our own *perestroika* of language teaching in schools in Britain. Here, central government and the DES have recognised the need for more Russian linguists and specialists in Soviet and East European affairs, and have declared their support for an enhanced investment in Russian teaching in schools. Government observations on the House of Commons Second Report on Soviet Studies (1986) stress that 'where possible schools should consider offering Russian as a first or second foreign language'. In the DES policy statement: *Modern Languages in the School Curriculum* (1988),[5] Russian is included with other European languages as eligible for diversification schemes.

At the same time as recognition of the national need to produce more Russian linguists, a number of positive, practical developments have taken place which will serve to promote this objective, and which have changed the whole scene of Russian teaching.

Educational contacts with the USSR

The idea that the Soviet Union is remote and inaccessible, offering few profitable opportunities for students to visit the country and use their Russian, is in this day and age a completely outdated myth. For example, did you know that in the summer of 1988 a party of Soviet schoolchildren from the historic city of Vladimir were staying with English families in Canterbury, on the return half of a home-to-home exchange visit? Pupils from the Simon Langton School had previously stayed with Russian families in Vladimir, and were certainly able to use their Russian to good effect. Or were you aware that Soviet trainee teachers of English from Siberia were boating on the river Wharfe in Yorkshire? Siberia is certainly distant, but no longer so remote. Tourists are now flocking to the USSR. And for many years thousands of British schoolchildren have visited Moscow and Leningrad on school trips.

The 'normalisation' of relations with the Soviet Union has led to the Secretary of State visiting Moscow and signing an agreement for school exchanges, involving 50 British schools and 2,000 pupils by the year 1991/2. Schools have seized upon this opportunity with alacrity, whether teaching Russian or not, and it is bound to be an enormous stimulus to the teaching of Russian in future. Russian can now compete on equal terms with other languages in opportunities for visits and exchanges. We shall now have lots of Russian schoolchildren visiting our towns and cities, staying with families. For several years there have been increasing contacts through student visits and delegations. Now there will be much wider scope for contacts with Russian people at a personal level, and in schools there will be wholly genuine reasons for teaching Russian for purposes of real-life communication.

Educational reasons for teaching Russian in schools, already strong from the point of view of the cultural diversity of the USSR, have now been enhanced at a stroke.

Teaching materials

The necessary teaching materials are available to ensure that learners acquire effective communication skills in Russian. The lack of suitable and attractive teaching materials for Russian has been much lamented in past years, but this no longer applies today.

In the first place, during the period when commercial firms were reluctant to publish materials for Russian, teachers of Russian have shown great initiative, enthusiasm and resource in cooperatively producing quality teaching materials of their own, closely related to the needs of the classroom. Outstanding examples of this are the *Pora* materials, compiled by the joint efforts of Scottish teachers through CRAMP (Communicative Russian Auxiliary Materials Project), and *Iskra*, produced by the Association of Nuffield Teachers of Russian, again through their own efforts, as an updated and improved replacement of the original *Vperyod!* materials.

It could in fact be said that the reluctance of firms to publish commercially has had a positive and beneficial effect, in providing the stimulus for cooperative teacher-based production of a whole range of ancillary teaching materials to meet particular teaching needs. Other materials like *Sdelai Sam, Eshcho Raz, Kaleidoskop, Govorit Moskva, Ya Pishu Vam,* the Firth Park Russian materials, and others, have been produced by practising teachers, demonstrated at national in-service courses for teachers of Russian held at the Universities of Sheffield and York, and made generally available at low cost.

Moreover, if teaching materials for Russian could not be published commercially in this country, they could in Moscow. The third national in-service course held at York in 1988 saw the arrival in the UK of the books for Part 2 of *Pervy Dialog*, impressively produced by the Moscow publishers Russky Yazyk.

Parts 1 and 2 of *Pervy Dialog* provide a large resource of modern, colourful and authentic teaching material for the early stages of learning Russian and through to GCSE. The course is based heavily on a communicative approach to learning Russian, and has been produced over a number of years by an Anglo-Soviet team of co-authors through a collaborative link between the Language Teaching Centre of the University of York, and A.S. Pushkin Russian Language Institute, Moscow. The materials are readily available to teachers through Collets, acting with Russky Yazyk as joint publishers and distributors.

The success of this project has led to the Association of Teachers of Russian initiating a further collaborative project with the Pushkin Institute for the production of additional communicative materials addressed to specific requirements of GCSE.

Soviet publishers have themselves produced a range of attractive and colourful teaching aids for English-speaking learners of Russian. As well as books, dictionaries, readers, background material, these also include video teaching materials – *Dobro pozhalovat*, humorous cartoon films produced by the Pushkin Institute. Further video materials on GCSE topics, 'Russian in Dialogues and Interviews', have been produced by Wolverhampton Polytechnic.

It simply cannot be said that there is a lack of teaching material for Russian. All these materials are available now.

David Rix and Robert Pullin

The York-Sheffield Russian Project

This project, grant-aided by the Nuffield Foundation, aims to support the consolidation and extension of Russian teaching in schools. It is currently supporting a national network of teacher-based materials development groups in the production of additional ancillary teaching materials to fill any gaps in teaching Russian to GCSE, and introductory or supplementary materials for 11 year old beginners' courses within the framework of the DES policy of diversification of first foreign language teaching. Main networks are in operation with centres in Birmingham, Edinburgh, Glasgow, London, Manchester, Oxford and Sheffield, with other linked sub-groups.

As well as providing a framework to assist teachers in producing additional new teaching materials, the project also aims to promote models of teacher development, and to help teachers prepare to meet the challenge of diversification and adjust to new demands of teaching Russian across the ability range. The process of collaborative materials production will facilitate the sharing of ideas and experience among teachers of Russian, often at present working in isolation in individual schools. A series of national and regional in-service courses will assist preparation for diversification. The project was launched at the third national in-service course for teachers of Russian on the theme of 'GCSE and diversification: meeting the needs', where the network groups were organised, in the autumn of 1988. A follow-up course for Russian teachers took place at York in April 1989, within the framework of a UGC funded INSET project on diversification based at the Language Teaching Centre of the University of York.

Through the regional networks, the project will also monitor, evaluate and publicise new developments and initiatives for the consolidation and extension of Russian teaching in secondary schools.

In the production of teaching materials some network groups are concentrating on meeting the needs of the new GCSE examination, while others are particularly keen to prepare for diversification and produce materials for teaching Russian to young mixed-ability learners. Published course books cannot be ideally suited to these particular needs, and a good stock of teacher-produced materials, visual aids and games, tried and tested in the classroom, is essential. Within the two-year span, the project aims to facilitate the production, publication and distribution of selected, validated materials in an inexpensive form.

Teacher training

In addition to a groundswell of new teaching materials, Russian is also fortunate in having enthusiastic teachers of high quality who can make a success of communicative language teaching, whether to first-form learners or to pupils opting for Russian as a second foreign language.

36

The new generation of Russian teachers are far better equipped to teach their language through oral, skill-oriented methods than ever before. For several years now, the majority of undergraduates studying Russian have taken opportunities to spend a lengthy period of study residence in the USSR during their degree course, usually from three months up to a full year. Postgraduates following a teacher training course, for example in centres at Nottingham, Sheffield and York, also have the opportunity of spending a further month on a study course in Leningrad during their PGCE year.

These new teachers of Russian are proficient speakers of the language, and have direct, first-hand knowledge and experience of contemporary life in the USSR. (A new trend in the past year or so has been to receive applications from graduates who have acquired a Russian husband while in the USSR!) The days when Russian was considered a 'special case' from the point of view of GCE oral examinations are long gone. The excellent grades achieved in the 1988 GCSE examination bear this out.

Graduates receive specialist training for teaching Russian, have a good understanding of methods and materials, and are all well equipped to undertake a communicative approach to teaching Russian in the classroom. They are not only committed to teaching Russian, but are also versatile – they can all offer French, and possibly German, as well as Russian.

To summarise at this point: we have a favourable climate of vastly improved relations with the USSR, increasing cultural and educational contacts, trade prospects, and Government recognition of the need for more Russian linguists; we have ample teaching materials, well-qualified teachers, and widening opportunities for school visits, exchanges and personal contacts to ensure the success of Russian teaching as an educational process; in these areas we have everything necessary to support the consolidation and extension of Russian teaching in schools as a first or second foreign language.

What is still needed is to publicise and make these positive developments and achievements more widely known, and to change old attitudes or misconceptions about the teaching of Russian.

The 'difficulty' of Russian

There is one main obstacle to be overcome if Russian is to feature in schemes for diversification, and that is the perception of Russian as a very difficult language. This is clearly illustrated by some of the teacher opinions expressed in the OXPROD publication, *Attitudes Towards Diversification*[6]:

'for the more able Russian is fascinating'
'Russian is probably best left until a later date because of the complexity of the language etc.'
'Russian could not be a mixed-ability language'

As another respondent to the OXPROD questionnaire wryly pointed out:

'old attitudes die hard'

It is a fact that in the past Russian has mostly (but not exclusively) been offered to the most linguistically gifted pupils as a second or third modern language, and possibly, in some cases, with considerable emphasis on a grammatical approach.

Russian does *not* have to be restricted to the academically gifted élite. The supposed difficulty of Russian is greatly exaggerated, particularly within the context of the current aims, objectives and methods of a communicative approach to modern languages teaching. *Anyone* in fact can learn to understand and speak Russian.

Mixed ability teaching: accessibility

Russian *can* be taught in schools to mixed ability classes. It *is* being taught to 11 or 12 year old learners across the ability range. Successful examples of this include Firth Park School, Sheffield; Castle Vale School, Solihull; St Benedict's School, Derbyshire; the Elizabethan High School, Retford; Armadale Academy in Scotland; and Fairwater Comprehensive in Wales.

David Rix has himself been teaching Russian to a first year mixed-ability class at Brayton High School, near Selby, since September 1988.

If we have to argue about relative difficulty, it could be said that at the introductory stage Russian is in some respects easier for young learners than other European languages. For Russian is essentially an economical language. There is, for example, no use of a present tense of the verb 'to be' in Russian. The verb 'to have' is conveyed by an idiomatic construction. (No-one can complain that pupils learning Russian do not know the present tense of 'to be' and 'to have' in Year 4!) There are no articles in Russian, and consequently no immediate problem with gender of nouns. The gender of nouns is in any case mostly clearcut and obvious in Russian. Asking questions, by intonation or question words, is simpler – there are no complexities of inversion or equivalents of *Est-ce que/Qu'est-ce que?* Above all, the verb system is economical in form, especially the past tense, and so it is possible to 'break in' to the language more easily.

As far as the sounds of Russian are concerned, young learners have good ears and are very quick to pick these up. There were no problems at all in the Brayton class with individual sounds. Certain sound combinations in particular words caused some difficulty, but the children are generally good mimics, and there have been no significant problems over pronunciation. Without wishing to make any kind of sweeping generalisation, it does seem that boys, in particular, find the pronunciation of Russian easier than French.

The Russian alphabet

And so to the Cyrillic alphabet, which is still commonly considered to be a terrible stumbling block to the learning of Russian. This view, we suppose, is inevitable, since to anyone who has not learned Russian a text in Cyrillic must look quite alien and inaccessible. (We might feel the same way about Chinese characters – how can anyone possibly learn them?)

After the initial weeks of oral work, however, all the Brayton first formers quickly picked up the letters of the handwritten Russian alphabet over six lessons in the couple of weeks before half term, through picture cards of known vocabulary and by playing games. It naturally takes longer for all pupils to be able to recognise, read, and write words and sentences, but this can be achieved gradually through puzzle-type worksheets. And with a first form class you have the time – the introduction of printed material can be deferred until later, when the pupils are fully familiar with handwritten script.

So, it cannot be over emphasised: the Russian alphabet, like the language as a whole, is not nearly as difficult as is supposed after all. There are a few pupils in David Rix's mixed-ability class who need additional learning support for their maths and English. They have all learned the Russian alphabet without too much trouble. And it was fun.

Those inflexions . . .

There are, of course, very real difficulties in learning Russian, as in any other language, for example, the fact that Russian has six cases and is a highly inflected language. If Russian is taught in a very analytical and cerebral way, it can provide as challenging and exasperating a course of study as anyone could conceivably wish for.

Sado-masochism apart, however, it does not have to be like that. In listening and speaking examples of all six cases have been used during the first term at Brayton High School with no apparent problems. The fact is that these young learners have little or no concept of grammar, accept without questioning, and are simply not bothered by inflexions. This does not, of course, mean 'pidgin Russian', but rather that pupils grow accustomed to inflexions gradually, through using the language.

The communicative approach, with its emphasis on conveying meaning rather than on form, and new GCSE examinations in which assessment is based on success in communicating a message rather than on strict grammatical accuracy, has had a particularly beneficial and liberating effect on Russian teaching.

We have dwelt on this area of 'difficulty' at some length, because it is clearly of such central and crucial importance to attitudes. If Russian continues to be perceived as 'too difficult' it cannot have a bright future in schools. The myth has to be demolished and swept away once and for all.

In fact, comparison of the relative ease or difficulty of learning French,

David Rix and Robert Pullin

German, Italian, Russian or Spanish is, in our view, not particularly productive. No language is 'easy' to learn. The only point that needs emphasis here is that Russian can be taught and learned in just the same way as any other language.

Mixed-ability teaching methods

For any language the degree of 'difficulty' and success in learning depend to a large extent on how it is taught, and this applies particularly to young mixed-ability classes, where methods are paramount. The approach clearly requires a strong emphasis on learning through the ears and learning through doing. Once trained to listen (not always easy to achieve!) all children in a mixed-ability class can make excellent progress in understanding spoken Russian.

For speaking they clearly need a lot of oral task-based activities, role playing, participation in pair work and group work, and games. They must have activities with a clear purpose or strong focal point of interest – other forms of 'language practice' are useless, and boring to them. The pupils demand variety and fun in lessons. They pick things up quickly, but need a whole variety of activities, tasks, visual aids, games to use material over and over again in different ways to achieve retention.

There are no short cuts, and any explanations involving grammatical terminology are simply out of the question. They like writing in Russian, provided the task is simple enough and there is again some point of interest, for example, filling in a puzzle-type worksheet. They will learn well if you give them something to do which involves using the language and which they find interesting.

This kind of approach with a young mixed-ability class, where the emphasis has to be on pupil-centred learning rather than teaching, may well require a good deal of adjustment on the part of a teacher not fully accustomed to it. Our young PGCE students, however, take to it like ducks to water. During part of the first autumn term they came into school with David Rix for Wednesday group work lessons. They soon took over the class and conducted the lessons themselves.

The approach certainly does require a lot of ideas and a good many teacher-produced materials for activities. This is where the York-Sheffield Project can help in facilitating the sharing of ideas and materials between teachers of Russian.

It should also be said that teaching Russian to a first year mixed-ability class, although demanding, can be very enjoyable and rewarding. The class at Brayton High School is making very creditable progress, and there is no reason why they should not all be able to tackle the North Yorks Level 1 graded test in Russian in the summer term.

For the less able pupils in the class a certificate in Russian will no doubt be a cause for considerable satisfaction and motivation. In subsequent years to GCSE there will clearly be a need for more emphasis on differentiated learning within the group.

Implementation: practical considerations

So far, this contribution has attempted to give good reasons why more Russian should be taught in our schools, to point out some of the positive developments which facilitate the teaching, and to show that Russian can be taught successfully as a first foreign language under diversification schemes, in just the same way as French, German, Italian or Spanish.

There remains the question as to how the consolidation and extension of Russian in schools can best be implemented from the practical and administrative aspects. This involves matters of parental attitude towards diversification, timetabling, resources and, above all, staffing.

The individual case of introduction of Russian into the first form at Brayton High School is perhaps interesting from the point of view of parental attitudes. This year one Russian class has been started for the first time, alongside two German and three French in a split year pattern. Letters were sent out to the parents of approximately 180 children informing them of the new arrangement for languages. Only six parents voiced strong feelings about which language their child should take, and of these one was strongly against Russian, and one strongly for. If this is typical, then parents' views of 'Which language?' do not loom large as a factor in diversification. Of course, parents previously had no choice anyway – all pupils had automatically learned French as a compulsory subject in the first year. There was clearly no need to 'sell' the idea of diversification to parents, nor the introduction of Russian.

With regard to timetabling, pupils have three hourly lessons a week for their first language in Year 1, and two hours a week in following years. From Year 2 they can take French or German as a second foreign language.

For the first year David Rix is producing his own teaching materials for Russian, and these will form part of the pool of materials produced by the York-Sheffield Project. North Yorks LEA has provided funds for the purchase of books for later years.

In the year 1989 to 1990 there will be four classes and a total of approximately 120 young learners of Russian in Years 1 and 2 at Brayton High School. Following the appointment of two teachers with Russian as well as French or German, there will be two new first form classes: introduction of Russian as a second foreign language for one class in Year 2; and the Year 2 continuation class. In this particular example of diversification the intention is to establish the teaching of Russian firmly in the school, alongside French and German.

LEA pilot schemes

Ten LEAs with an Education Support Grant are currently preparing pilot schemes for diversification. First indications are that within these schemes provision for Russian is likely to be highly variable. The Birmingham LEA pilot scheme, for example, is very encouraging, and proposes that Russian should feature in diversification plans in five schools, on a split year model from 11+, except in one school where Russian will be taught as a second language from 12+. In other LEAs proposals to extend the teaching of Russian to larger numbers of pupils as a second foreign language are also to be welcomed. In other cases diversification will be restricted exclusively to German and Spanish, and the outlook for Russian, or Italian, is decidedly bleak.

Teacher supply

It is apparent that the chief question for Russian is the availability of teachers. It is clearly easier to include Russian as a first foreign language, or extend it as a second, in those schools where it is already taught, or where teachers of Russian already exist.

Published DES figures on the employment of full-time teachers with qualifications in languages for England and Wales indicate that Russian has the largest number of 'unused' or 'underused' teachers. Only about 20% of teachers qualified in Russian are actually teaching the language at present. It is known for example, that Staffordshire pilot LEA has fourteen teachers with a qualification in Russian (A level or degree subsidiary) who are not teaching the language.

The DES is currently considering refresher courses for the pool of 'unused' qualified teachers, and the provision of incentives to retrain would make sound economic and educational sense. This could serve both to assist the extension of Russian teaching, and perhaps also help to diminish the acute problem of the shortage of teachers of French and other languages needed to meet the requirements of languages in the National Curriculum, at a time when Eric Hawkins and Gordon Lawrence[7] have drawn attention to the decline in the number of languages graduates, and referred to modern languages teachers as 'an endangered species'.

Russian as first or second foreign language: possibilities

There is a very strong case for Russian to be taught as a first foreign language in those schools where there is a clear will to do so, and where it proves possible. To teach Russian from the first form to large numbers of pupils at least two teachers of Russian are needed, as illustrated in the successful establishment of Russian at Wolverhampton High School for Girls.

The existence of more than one teacher of Russian in a school also helps to avoid possible problems of continuity of staffing. It is clear that present teacher supply, even with a high proportion of 'unused' teachers returning to Russian, is not sufficient to enable Russian to be taught as a first foreign language on any large scale, but it should permit a Russian presence in the majority of LEAs.

Indications of a trend towards teaching Russian to larger numbers of pupils as a second foreign language from the second or third year are encouraging. It is hoped that this will lead to more pupils studying Russian in the sixth form to A level, and continuing at university. Professor Pockney, in his inaugural lecture at the University of Surrey[8], has made a powerful case for the crucial need to produce more graduates in Russian. A stronger base of Russian teaching in schools, as well as *ab initio* courses at university, is necessary to achieve this.

In turn, more graduates in Russian will be needed to train as teachers in order to sustain consolidation and extension of Russian in schools. Russian teaching needs to be strengthened and grow to the point where it can reach a viable and stable position in schools, readily maintain its teaching force, and avoid problems of continuity and pupil mobility which have been apparent in the past.

If a stronger base of Russian teaching in schools can be created and sustained now, there is hope that in the longer term it will be possible for Russian to be available in at least one school in every LEA as a first or second foreign language, and in large LEAs in at least one school in each cluster of schools.

The need for Russian

In emphasising the need for a national capability in languages, the DES policy statement on diversification clearly looks to the single European market of 1992 and recommends that on the question of 'Which languages?' priority should be given to the main languages of the European Community.

While no-one would dispute this, it would be short-sighted to ignore prospects of increased trade with the vast market of Eastern Europe and the USSR. Professor Wade of Strathclyde University has pointed to the enormous potential for trade with the USSR, and the need for a knowledge of Russian for those who seek to tap this market and achieve profitable economic goals beyond the bounds of the EC.[9]

Whether on economic, political, cultural, scientific or educational grounds, the Soviet Union today cannot be ignored, and there is every reason to strengthen the teaching of Russian in our schools and universities.

Russian has come of age

In terms of an enthusiastic and well-qualified teaching force, modern teaching materials and methods, exciting possibilities for contacts with the USSR, we have everything necessary to do the job successfully, and make Russian teaching in schools a valuable educational experience.

Times have changed radically. Russian is no longer the 'poor relation' or a 'special case'. Teachers of Russian are justifiably proud of their achievements, consider that the teaching of Russian deserves a higher profile in schools, and that it is now timely for Russian to be accepted as a normal modern language along with French, German, Italian and Spanish.

Diversification provides the stimulus and opportunity for consolidation and extension of Russian in schools to take place. This time the opportunity should be taken, and followed through.

5

Spanish – At Last?

Sonia Rouve

The title echoes – with intention and indebtedness – that of Allison Peers's seminal work *Spanish – Now.*[1] It reflects the hope of Hispanists that, perhaps, 'now' may be becoming actuality, some 45 years after the first publication of Peers's clarion call.

I shall contend that, despite the setbacks and lack of success which Spanish has so often encountered, the arguments for teaching it are, and have always been, sound ones, and that now, entering the 1990s, we might just begin to see its flowering, assisted by recently formulated and widely agreed policies for language teaching.[2] But here the point needs to be firmly made with regard to the terms of reference of this volume, and as indeed is argued elsewhere, that neither Spanish nor any of the 'languages other than French' stand likely to benefit if the proper order is not observed: policies for the 'diversification' of modern language teaching *must* precede the implementation of the fine print of the National Curriculum.

It is surely widely agreed that 'languages other than French could be introduced more frequently as first foreign languages, either on their own or as alternatives to French'[3] and that 'the Language Associations in general welcome this document with its encouragement to diversify language provision'[4]. It follows that, if a sound basis of diversified provision is not established, the National Curriculum, delaying the introduction of a second foreign language 'until the fourth year'[5], may well see the continued domination of French. So, 'diversification' and 'the National Curriculum', in that order.

Is it not, however, rather depressing to be setting out the same facts, the same justification, 45 years after Peers? Of course it is, but would that it was only for that length of time that Spanish had been missing out. The facts, most of them, have been around for a lot longer, and so have similar justifications. It is these same facts which we must put into a contemporary context and attempt finally to see a rational policy of modern language education implemented; a policy where no one language dominates, for 'there is no "first language" in life',[6] but where proper thought is given to the reasons for teaching languages.

Historical overview

Let it not be thought that the publication of *Spanish – Now* in 1944 was the first time the case for Spanish had been put; indeed it could be said that it was a growing impatience with the frequency – but lack of success – with which the case had been put, that spurred the publication of the book.

A glance at the early teaching of languages in Britain will serve to highlight the changing fortunes of Spanish. Let us not think, however, that the lack of any decisive policy with regard to languages other than French, which perhaps peaked in that decade of disenchantment, the 1970s, marks some descent from a 'golden age' when Spanish fared better. Far from it: before the First World War Spanish was hardly taught in this country at all, either in schools or in universities. This in itself is perhaps hardly surprising when one recalls that even in the late eighteenth century it was only very occasionally, and then only in the 'dissenting Academies', that French was taught (still alongside, and not in place of, Latin). This innovation, albeit on a very minor scale, does have current implications to which I shall return: French was taught by the influx of native speaker refugees, many of whom were scholars in their own right, from the French Revolution. Latin only very gradually began to relinquish its pre-eminent position as the language which offered the best mental discipline, and although the seventeenth, and increasingly the eighteenth, centuries saw the spread of French as a diplomatic language and of English as that of scientific papers, the grammar schools, limited by their statutes, retained Latin. It was also guaranteed a place as the language of religion.

Early nineteenth-century attempts to vary the terms of school charters to allow the introduction of 'modern studies' were unsuccessful.[7] It was this view of the cerebral value of Latin (vernacular languages had of course been taught since the Middle Ages for use by merchants) which persisted well into the last century.

It was the Victorian period which saw the great awakening of interest in 'modern' languages (though taught, of course, by 'classical' means and, indeed, by classics masters). The work of the notable Commissions (Newcastle, Clarendon) of the 1860s, led to reform of the curriculum, for both the poorer and the richer classes. Concurrently with the gradual introduction of French, the period saw the rise of the teaching of German, in great part due to the prestige of the thinkers and writers of the nineteenth century. Taught often as an extra, a 'modern' language could hardly be said to enjoy an assured place in the curriculum.

And so the time finally came for French, then for German; and what of Spanish? It could be said that, *grosso modo*, until 1936 Spain was spared such major political upheavals with pan-European reverberations and had, therefore, in the mind of British educationists enjoyed a quiet, very low-profile existence.

With the dawning of a new century, let us now look at the dawning interest in a new language of potential educational value: how fares Spanish in the twentieth century? What lessons can we learn from its position and progress over nearly a century? What possibilities are there for the future?

Spanish in the twentieth century

It has been earlier stated that before the First World War hardly any Spanish was taught. In such a vacuum, therefore, there came a novel statement made in the Board of Education's memorandum on modern language teaching issued in 1912, that there were:

> strong utilitarian reasons why an opportunity should be given for learning Spanish . . . in selected schools in districts having a considerable trade with countries [where Spanish is spoken]

and that

> the Board would favourably consider any proposal for [its] introduction into the curriculum under suitable conditions where it is shown that a real demand . . . exists.[8]

It is hardly surprising, however, if such a heavily-qualified invitation found few takers (Spanish for the merchants again). Even in Liverpool, often quoted as an active centre of Spanish teaching and University base of the great Allison Peers, there were, in 1920, only two schools offering the language and, before 1914, there were probably no more than a dozen in the whole country. After the war, and partly as a reaction against German, a new second language was looked for. The obvious choice was Spanish and it was adopted by over 100 schools. (It is a mark of the shaky position of 'languages other than French' that, in the years preceding national surveys – of the kind undertaken by the Schools Council or ATSP – and the development of the DES Research and Statistics department, very few specific facts can be elucidated. It was until recently the same, for example, for examination entries and GTTR figures: 'other languages'). Figures, if lacking detail, nevertheless increase, albeit slowly. By 1934 Spanish figured in the curriculum (often as an 'extra' subject) of 250 schools. In his *Handbook to the Study and Teaching of Spanish* Allison Peers (writing, interestingly, just before the Spanish Civil War and in a mood of sadly temporary euphoria) states that:

> it is unnecessary nowadays to quote figures in support of the contention that Spanish, as a subject of study, is steadily gaining in popularity . . . . Over 300 secondary schools either teach it regularly or present pupils in it at public examinations.[9]

He is nevertheless cautious in his Preface to this perhaps not so widely known or acknowledged earlier work, for he writes '[The study of Spanish] in our schools is at present too empirical to be entirely satisfactory'.[10]

The *Handbook*, it may be noted, was 'published now in readiness for the forward movement in the study of Spanish which the end of the [Civil] war can hardly fail to bring . . .'.[11]

Despite strong arguments that more Spanish be taught ('The chief need is that the amount of Spanish being taught should greatly increase'[12]), a decline can be noted from 1936, which can be attributed, at least partially, to the Civil

Figure 1

Examining bodies

Languages	Oxford Local			Cambridge Local		
	1938	1939	1941	1938	1939	1941
French	11,156	11,683	10,378	7,688	7,686	7,839
Spanish	84	106	64	111	76	53

Languages	Oxford and Cambridge Schools Exam. Board			Joint Matriculation Board			University of London
	1938	1939	1941	1938	1939	1941	1941
French	8,600	8,746	7,042	20,486	21,336	19,275	14,168
Spanish	271	210	100	284	292	273	232

War which not only effectively closed the country to teachers and pupils, but also had its effect on attitudes. This decline continued through the Second World War, compounded now by a shortage of teachers. Figures for School Certificate examination entries for these years show not only the relative drop in numbers taking Spanish but, as ever, its position relative to French.

With reference to the figures for French, Allison Peers asks:

Can anyone maintain that such a disproportion serves the best interests either of the pupil or of the community? Dare anyone assert that ... French is 100 times as important ... as Spanish?

Is it not the duty of anyone who considers the disproportion excessive to do what he can to reduce it?[13]

A consideration of such issues will shortly be undertaken. Let it first be said, however, that, just as when Allison Peers was reviewing the period from the First World War to the brink of the Second and was dismayed, we are now able to review the decades since the last war with more optimism: Spanish has regained the lost ground and examination entries have been constantly, if slowly, on the increase. It has not equalled German as a 'second foreign language'[14] but has, especially recently, developed in some extremely encouraging ways.

Arguments for the inclusion of Spanish

No review of the 'facts' of the history of modern language teaching in this country can stand without a consideration of the factors which have been thought to influence the situation.

Mention has been briefly made of early arguments of utility, particularly with regard to trade and commerce, but, while this could be supported in some circles, it could hardly be a major argument for the inclusion of *any* language in an educational context. Indeed, it should perhaps be said that, on educational grounds, two points need first to be made: that the most urgent need is to do away altogether with the idea that one foreign language (i.e. French) should be the dominant one and secondly that, allowing the educational benefit to be derived from freeing oneself from the monoglot prison by learning another language, a case could be made for any one of a range of languages.

Let us therefore address the particular arguments in favour of Spanish. Allison Peers adumbrates four 'cases' when asking 'what should be the intrinsic qualities of a modern foreign language that is to be widely taught in schools . . . not only as a "second" or a "third" language, but also as a first language?'.[15] They are: educational, cultural, political and commercial. They are all valid, but need expanding. Accessibility and relevance are helpful concepts here.

The 'educational' case has, over the years, been made on the accessibility of Spanish, i.e. its relative linguistic facility. Spanish represents:

(1) phonetic simplicity	an important consideration as regards oral work.
(2) orthographic regularity	facilitates written work and allows for the introduction of reading at an early stage. A real bonus in the classroom as it means a greater variety of activity can be introduced from an early stage.
(3) morphological and syntactic simplicity	

It also has simpler rules of gender classification; tense formation and structure are similar to English (in Mackey's terms, therefore, there is less 'distance'), and the formation of the interrogative, so important for classroom situations, is regular.[16] Of course, 'Spanish grammar is incredibly rich in complexities and can test the abilities of any pupil. However, without distorting the realities of the language too much, it is possible to reserve the really testing areas of grammar to a relatively late stage (e.g. Years 3 or 4)'.[17]

Accessibility or 'linguistic facility' has, of course, proved a two-edged sword: if not a 'mental discipline', then it is for the 'least able', and consequently afforded little real respect. Indeed, with the egalitarian ideals of the 1960s and a policy of a modern language for all pupils, came good and bad effects for Spanish. 'Good' because it picked up some numbers where French was thought 'too difficult'; 'bad' because the label 'for the least able' stuck.

With the criterion of relevance in mind, we may turn to a consideration of the other points, taking the socio-cultural next. With the linguistic emphasis now so firmly centred on developing communicative competence, not only is it the case that Spanish allows as much if not more rapid progress here than some other languages, but it can be geared to 'communication in the country' since of the four million British who holiday annually in Spain, a good proportion of our pupils must be among them. And that is excluding the school journeys and exchanges which are undertaken. The world's third most widely spoken language (and we have, as yet, not even touched on Latin America), combined with Europe's most visited holiday destination makes for a powerfully relevant argument.

On the question of cultural and historical attraction, few countries (again, without crossing the Atlantic) can claim the rich and fascinating heritage of Spain, going far beyond the 'tourist' bull-fight or 'flamenco evening'; ancient Mozarabic architecture or avant-garde film and music, and painting of all periods, cater for all ages and tastes.

The argument for the inclusion of Spanish in the modern language curriculum becomes even stronger when we do – finally – address the areas of Central and South (Latin) America. Here, while the 'holiday' argument may recede, the cultural, historical, political and commercial arguments all come to the fore. Study of Spanish opens up, literally, a whole New World of experience: whether that of the explorers and discoverers, of the rich indigenous civilisations and their history and archaeology, the lively literary figures of that continent, or the politics of central and South America; all are worthy areas of study (and are increasingly appearing in re-structured A level syllabuses).

'Latin America' and 'markets' are terms which recur and in conjunction.[18] Here too (not to mention Spain's fairly recent inclusion in the European Community, to be followed by 'open frontiers' in 1992) we see that oft-quoted commercial argument and, although now not presenting quite such a gloomy picture, the British Overseas Trade Board noted in 1979 that 'less English is spoken by Spanish businessmen than in probably any other major market in Western Europe'.[19] It is still, however, true that 'any company using English, or with literature not in Spanish, starts off at a very serious disadvantage'.

This is surely a convincing enough set of arguments for Spanish taking its rightful place. (What, and how exactly, that may be will be expanded on). In addition, however, one more argument from experience, deserves to be quoted. Eric Hawkins, reflecting on his own adolescence, writes:

> I cannot be the only Protestant schoolboy who learned from Fray Luis de León a view of Catholicism very different from that peddled by the rival marchers in Liverpool in the '20s.[20]

Spanish for tolerance and understanding. Not a bad claim!

Post-war developments

We left the review of events at the immediate post-war period. We should now look to see how the reform of education (the 1944 Education Act, the Crowther Report, etc.), together with socio-political decisions (reorganisation of the school system in the 1960s along comprehensive lines) and the range of arguments determining modern language teaching, resulted in any change of the *status quo ante*.

Important dates and events for Spanish in this context include the foundation, in 1943, of the Hispanic Council, a union of interests brought about with the aim of stimulating and promoting the study of the Spanish language and of the countries in which it is spoken. A practical outcome of this foundation was the setting up of courses to train the large numbers of teachers which it was deemed would be necessary to meet post-war demand.

The recommendations of the Hispanic Council were incorporated into the Norwood Report[21] and bear stating:

(a) As new secondary schools are founded, Spanish should be adopted as the first (or only) modern language in a great number of them.

(b) In secondary schools where two languages are aimed at Spanish should, in a considerable number of cases, be the first language studied. In every large urban area there should be at least one school in which Spanish is the first language.

(c) Pupils of high linguistic capacity should be encouraged . . . to study Spanish . . .

(d) Such schools as are able . . . to switch over to Spanish as first language, or to introduce it as a second language, should be given every encouragement to do so.

How happy would today's Spanish teachers be if these had been implemented.

However, something else of great note was instituted: in 1947, no doubt arising out of the meetings of teachers under the auspices of the Hispanic Council, The Association of Teachers of Spanish and Portuguese (ATSP) of Great Britain was founded. The three main aims of the ATSP were:

(1) To promote . . . the study of Spanish and Portuguese in Great Britain.

(2) To foster . . . a knowledge of the culture of Spanish and Portuguese speaking peoples and to promote living contact with these people.

(3) To make a practical study at all stages of the problems affecting the teaching of Spanish . . .

The Chairman for 1947–48, stated:

We want to be able to speak with an authoritative voice for teachers . . . necessity of Hispanic Studies now firmly established . . . We intend to be an active Association and . . . meetings will deal with practical aspects of teaching at every level . . . survey textbooks . . . and pass on information about Hispanic cultural and educational activities abroad.[22]

The Hispanic Council's vacation course for that year represented a departure from previous courses in that it:

> gave instruction ... also in methods of Teaching Spanish. Mr B N Parker, of the Institute of Education, lectured on 'The principles of Language Teaching with special reference to Spanish' and discussion groups exchanged ideas on practical Spanish teaching problems.[23]

Reading through early issues of *Vida Hispánica* is fascinating and instructive. All the ideas are there. Looking back 40 years the intervening scene is not as bleak as it was for Allison Peers in 1944, but it still makes one want to say: 'No, not Spanish – some time; Spanish – here and there; Spanish – when and where entirely convenient to all concerned[24], but more of it, in more schools and now.

The expansionist Sixties

Modern language teachers entered the 1960s on the crest of the Crowther wave, calling for 'rethinking the whole basis of the teaching of languages in schools'.[25] It is difficult now to believe that so many developments took place in that boom decade: the first school language laboratory was installed; the tape recorder had become commonplace – for use with materials developed by the pioneering Nuffield Foreign Language Materials Project (the Nuffield Foundation, indeed backed the publication of a seminal work on methodology, *Modern Languages in the Grammar School*, which argued the case for 'communication' as the true aim of foreign language study); in 1953 the CSE 'an examination different in kind'[26] was introduced; language advisers began to be appointed; in 1965 CILT was set up. ... Nowadays we perhaps take the hard work of the pioneers of the 1960s very much for granted, but it is a decade to which modern language teachers must be forever grateful.

Were there, however, altogether too many goodies? We were certainly spoilt for opportunities, but all this expansion took place with no commonly agreed policy as to where we should be heading; it was 'experimental', but with no 'control'; there was so much to choose from: new methods, and splendid audio-visual materials crying *¡Adelante!*; new forms of examination, with a much higher proportion of the marks given for the spoken language; and, again in a fairly haphazard way, quite a lot of Spanish. Piecemeal, however, as the teacher, the materials or the mood dictated. But, if the teacher left (they so often did), the materials did not suit (and *Nos ponemos en camino* was still being used in a high proportion of schools) or the head decided on something else ... Spanish disappeared again.

Vida Hispánica is, as ever, a rich source of information regarding the empirical position of Spanish at this time. December 1960 saw the first of the Canning House conferences for teachers of Spanish, and discussions at that time were concerned in the main with performance in the GCE and with university entrance. Interestingly, it was noted that 'the increasing popularity of Russian ... was strengthening the competition against Spanish for a place on the school curriculum'. *O tempora* . . . Challenging editorials kept teachers of Spanish on their toes: 'Do we need a new concept of O level . . . largely oral in nature?'; 'Our pupils are learning Spanish . . . to be able to speak and write it, [so] works written before the [second] half of the nineteenth century cannot be usefully studied until a very late stage . . . it is a question of putting first things first . . . we should live in our own world first, that of current language use . . . through teacher, tape recorder, television and textbooks'.

A forward-looking article by Christine Roberts on the CSE argues the 'strong case for Spanish' and enjoins teachers to 'emerge from the GCE stronghold to join forces with the CSE pioneers . . . else, in some areas it may be overlooked', and 'make it realistic . . . for CSE examinees to "use their Spanish" '. The Editor joins the call for new materials: publishers 'let them not imagine that Spanish teachers are too backward-looking to provide them with . . . a market'. Methodology, too, began to take its rightful place: 'The Modern Approach to Language Teaching' discussed the language laboratory and drills; Ariza argues the case for Spanish occupying 'a more favourable place than . . . at the moment. . . . It is an eminently suitable language to be studied by a large proportion of the school population.'

To what extent were these views and hopes implemented? 1963 saw the first of a developing series of fact-gathering exercises: a survey of the teaching of Spanish in secondary schools. The enquiry found that, 'of 1550 replies received, Spanish formed a part of the curriculum in some 700', and 'as many as 83 . . . already teach Spanish as a first language'. Comprehensive reorganisation was intended to offer the widest range of subjects, with the corollary that Spanish might be offered as a genuine first language, not just as a second for the linguistically able or an 'easy alternative for the weaker pupils'. We read, too, of a very interesting pattern in a 'thirteen-form entry, fully comprehensive, school . . . [where] Spanish is a major language, taught initially to the same extent as French', and where 'the bottom block sets [have had] success in terms of enjoyment and achievement'. With 'three full-time and one part-time Spanish teachers . . . a language assistant . . . language laboratories' the Thomas Bennett School enjoyed excellent conditions. Another reason for 'the success of Spanish . . . is the use of *¡Adelante!*'.[27]

Finally, it seems, sailing on the expansionist tide of the 1960s Spanish is on course. What reefs can have lain ahead that now, approaching the 1990s, we are still desperately making the same plea: 'More Spanish - now!' What happened was the Seventies.

The disenchanted Seventies

The 1960s boom soon turned to gloom and doom in the 1970s. Just as in the expansionist 1960s, it did not happen all at once. However, the language laboratory (even when it worked) was seen *not* to be the panacea for all language learning ills; Primary French was *not* going to lead to an expansion of other languages at secondary level; comprehensive reorganisation did *not* always have such positive outcomes for language study as we saw at Thomas Bennett; despite their best efforts, teacher training establishments found they could *not* supply numbers of qualified teachers of Spanish (and, in a decentralised system, certainly could *not* deploy the teachers to the schools and areas where they might be most needed); partial provision without policy could *not* maintain the impetus.

Already in 1972 the Schools Council Modern Languages Project report on Spanish teaching in the United Kingdom adopted the ironically questioning title, *Stands Spanish where it should?*[28] Indeed, the generally held view was that it did *not*, despite the fact that, in absolute terms, the CSE had attracted more and more entries (e.g. from 235 in 1965 to 2,011 in 1970). This could be said to indicate satisfaction that at last we had an examination more appropriate to the wider range of ability pupils studying Spanish.

The previous year the President of the Association of British Hispanists had written to the Universities Council for the Education of Teachers (UCET) expressing concern over 'the critical situation in . . . universities . . . for the provision of special post-graduate courses for intending teachers of Spanish' and urged 'the creation . . . of further lectureships for specialists in Spanish'.[29] It is sad to reflect that of the five university departments of education then offering Spanish, four no longer do, and much retrospective credit must go, for example, to John MacNair and Hedley Sharples. UCET does not seem to have responded, though at King's College, London, the challenge was accepted and, in a still policy-less age as regards teacher education, it remains one of the few.[30]

It is worth picking out some of the brave local initiatives of the 1970s. George Varnava at Holland Park (twelve-form entry) comprehensive school in the ILEA was a proponent of curricular balance allied to economy of resources. While French predominated, four other languages were offered as options. It was decided to introduce Spanish and German in Year 1, each to three sets (i.e. 50% of the intake). This resulted in more stable groups continuing to Years 3 and 4.

A more radical experiment was attempted by Michael Marland at Woodberry Down School (ILEA). He had expressed concern over the administration, achievement – and indeed arbitrariness – of teaching two equal first languages, in itself unusual, and decided, after consultation with the modern languages inspectorate and King's, to change to Spanish as the first (and therefore, given options, effectively for the majority of pupils the *only*) foreign language to be taught. Thought, teacher power and money for materials were all expended in the planning and implementation of what remained, however, a one-off. (It may be mentioned at this point that the school of which Marland is currently Head, has been equally forward-looking, adopting one of the patterns of the 1980s: 'carousel' or 'taster' courses).

Discussion of the 1970s cannot conclude without mention of two seminal events, one for modern languages in general, the other Spanish-specific. 1977 saw the publication of *Modern Languages in Comprehensive Schools*, a study of 83 schools which found that 'the learning of modern foreign languages could be significantly improved [with] a more rational distribution of opportunities'.[31] The predominant position of French was, yet again, noted (e.g. in the sample of 83 schools, for 81 pupils taking French in Year 1, only five took Spanish); fractionally more pupils took Spanish than German in Year 1 (5:4), but Spanish showed no growth over Years 1–5. Only one school in the sample 'introduced French and Spanish as the first modern language in alternative years', even though many felt that 'too late a start is a severe handicap'.[32] Here we have some definite findings (and the beginnings of policy guidelines?). In 1978 one LEA followed up the implications with a message regarding 'training the teachers' that has certainly been adopted at King's: 'the importance of offering two languages . . . [this] will lead to an increase in flexibility for modern languages departments in schools'.[33] ILEA had, during the 1970s, effectively put money where its printed statements lay: the development of one of the first multi-media Spanish courses, *¡Claro!*, designed for the wide range of ability to whom, increasingly, Spanish was to be offered in its schools. The success of *¡Claro!* was not long overlooked by publishers, previously unconvinced of the commercial value of Spanish courses.

In 1978, the ATSP decided it was the moment to 'fly the flag' and, together with the Association of Hispanists, it organised the first colloquium on the teaching of Spanish in the United Kingdom. Concerns addressed by speakers included the supply of specialist teachers, the availability of Spanish language materials, and the general need to improve the flow of information about the full range of courses available to school leavers. Participants (some 200, hosted by the Instituto de España) were conscious that Spanish teaching in the 1980s would have to live through a time of educational and economic change but that 'the challenges ahead could be faced with optimism'.[34]

Into the Eighties – questioning and planning

Perhaps it is a feature of eternal human optimism to believe that – at last – one has got it right, but it certainly does seem that, by *questioning* past practice and an increasing trend towards *planning* the future (1987 and 1988 saw the publication of important policy statements with regard to modern language teaching, which go a bit further, too, than the traditional 'advice'; terms such as 'should' and 'it is recommended' are now used),[35] we *may* be on track. By questioning, we were sharpening the focus, and the focus was fixed on 'diversification'.

Here it is perhaps worth noting that, since terminology may affect practice or vice versa, all the discussions, reports etc. on the place of languages other than French have, until very recently, adopted the particular focus of 'the *second* foreign language'. Many have been the proposals for shifting or reversing the order etc. of languages taught in schools, but it has always been a basically *ordinal* approach.[36] It was a natural extension of work on second foreign languages 'to begin to take an interest in diversification of first foreign language provision'.[37] The notion of 'diversification' liberates our thinking to a certain extent and encourages positive consideration of the curricular possibilities.

Indeed, as has been mentioned earlier, 'diversification' is *the* key issue and must needs be addressed first if the National Curriculum is to be sensibly implemented as regards modern languages. Concern with the concept has been gradually building: 'the notion that adequate diversification of foreign language teaching can be achieved through second or third language courses . . . has proved illusory',[38] to be explored for the first time in any depth and detail in an important study of the early 1980s, *Languages other than French in the Secondary School*,[39] considered as *first or equal first foreign language*. The study, by a working party of the Schools Council Modern Languages Committee, derived from a concern that the continued dominance of French was threatening the position of other, or 'second' foreign languages, but this negative factor gave rise to the positive proposal of 'diversification of the first language'. Twenty-three case study schools were examined in detail and show a range of language combinations. Among the reasons offered for a change from French, the four which rank highest could (and do) relate to Spanish:[40]

Ease of learning the language	16
Availability of staff	13
Availability of resources	11
Appeal of the language to the pupils	10

The responses to the survey have served as the basis for much work on diversification, to result, most recently, in a fascinating survey of 'attitudes towards diversification'[41] compiled by members of the Oxford Project on Diversification of First Foreign Language Teaching (OXPROD) team. The implications for the teaching of Spanish of OXPROD are evident, and it is instructive to study the responses of language teachers in the Project schools. They were very positive: 'I think that diversification is very beneficial . . . pupils do not see their foreign language in isolation'. To questions regarding 'which language?' the answers are equally encouraging for, while there was obviously support for German, teachers also opted for Spanish as 'the most suitable first foreign language, . . . because of the ease with which it can be acquired', and also for relevance: 'most children are now more likely to visit Spain . . . [this] can be used for motivation'. Scoring of responses led to German (46) and Spanish (45) being perceived as the 'leading contenders for the language deemed . . . most suitable'.[42]

It was the ATSP's conviction that the limited (in terms of scale) findings of the Hadley Report plus the tantalising glimpses of available yet currently unused teachers of Spanish (that 'pool of teachers with languages other than French as main subjects of highest qualification . . . not engaged in teaching those languages'[43]), gave grounds for undertaking a major survey. This 'facts of Spanish' exercise was undertaken during the summer term 1984 via questionnaires to schools in every LEA, and to independent schools, where Spanish was taught. A total of 823 schools responded, giving a picture of Spanish provision across the country.[44] While not a complete list, it almost certainly represents the large majority of schools in which Spanish is taught.

The answers to the *questions* provide a rational base for *planning*. The facts to be derived from an analysis of the categories of response will therefore now be examined since they form a powerful set of arguments for the balanced inclusion of Spanish in a diversified language curriculum.

Schools and their languages

Twenty-three schools (22 state, one independent) reported Spanish as first foreign language (FL1), 32 as first equal foreign language (FL1=). Spanish was FL2 in over half of the schools where it is taught and FL3 in over a third (36%). With the proviso of assured staffing, Spanish appears fairly secure where two or three languages are offered, and this fact in itself provides a strong argument for diversification and balance. It would make obvious sense if the numbers of schools where Spanish is taught as FL1 or FL1= were increased.

The size of a school is obviously *one* factor in deciding language policy. However, where other circumstances are favourable, small size does not seem to militate against the inclusion of Spanish for, although three of those offering Spanish as FL1 had 1500 pupils on roll, a total of seven schools had fewer than 750. Of those offering Spanish as FL1=, five had 900 pupils, yet ten had fewer (400–800). The patterns are repeated when we look at the more established teaching of Spanish as FL2: the majority is in schools with fewer than 900 pupils. Small – or smallish – *can* be beautiful, it seems, and efficient. We need to ask why more of the larger schools are not doing the same. Since large size is often advanced as a necessary condition for curricular spread, let the larger schools deliver the goods!

In the context of schools being encouraged to diversify, it is heartening to note the continuing appointment of language advisers with Spanish-specific interests and qualifications. Two examples may serve to illustrate: close collaboration in the York area has led to a very healthy development in research (LTC-Nelson), materials (*¡Vaya!*) and courses ('Diversification', December 1988) in support of Spanish. In ILEA the modern languages inspectorate guided the progress and funded the publication of the hugely successful *¡Claro!* course. Current work in the ten areas awarded Education Support Grants (ESG) will further advance the cause of diversification.

Pupils and patterns

The ATSP survey allows us to see what the pupils are doing as well as when and how they are doing it. While in the largest group (291 schools), pupils begin Spanish in Year 3, a considerable number (20%) start to learn the language in Year 2. The pupils in the 74 schools where Spanish is introduced in Year 1 are, very possibly, being offered 'taster' courses. This system of a 'carousel' of three or four languages introduced in the first year of secondary schooling, and the final choice of language(s) to be studied delayed until Year 2, is one which has met with very mixed reactions and may or may not ultimately serve the cause of diversification.

How many pupils are studying Spanish in the different years, and for what proportion of their time? In 49 schools there were between 100 and 150 pupils learning Spanish in Years 1–3, an important stage for any policy of diversification. The weekly amount of time devoted to Spanish through to Year 5 was, in the main, two hours and 20 minutes – or something like three 45-minute periods – a decent amount of established teaching which could form a basis for the development of a rational policy of diversification.

Staff

Apart from the pupils engaged in learning Spanish, who is doing the work of persuading and organising? As ever, it is the committed and devoted teachers (often with a language other than Spanish as their main language of qualification), for whom the vision of a more broadly based language curriculum may yet become a reality.

In 83% of the schools there were one or two members of staff teaching Spanish, though in more than half the schools (434) the Spanish fort was held by a single teacher and this is obviously a worrying fact, for not only is that teacher working in professional isolation, but if she (as it so often is) should leave, the subject is totally at the mercy of the vast range of other curricular interests. While we may never aspire to the luxury, reported by one school, of having nine members of staff teaching Spanish, policy will best be implemented by sound staffing arrangements.

One of the most wasteful uses of resources confirmed in this survey was the famous untapped 'pool of teachers' with unused Spanish teaching potential currently working in schools.[45] In 1984 20% of schools reported at least one 'unused' teacher of Spanish, while a further 84 reported having more than one. This is a terrible waste of a valuable national resource. For years now, initial teacher training establishments have been preaching the advantage to schools of employing teachers able to offer two languages, but in the cold light of everyday reality, the lesser-taught language has stayed just that, and even been allowed to wither away. Policies (leading to lack of practice) and promotions (and consequent lack of time) are the most common causes. Properly planned, there is the potential for a massive increase in Spanish in schools.

Planning is what the ESG, GRIST and INSET proposals are all about. Pinpointing the specific needs of teachers of languages other than French, a recent National Foundation for Educational Research (NFER) survey[46] tells us what the situation is and, importantly, what the teachers say they need to up-date their rusty language skills ready to meet the challenge of doing more. An alternative to the (perhaps ideal) spending of time in the country was to:

> spend time on an intensive language course, preferably one designed specifically for teachers who wanted to revive a dormant language. Such a course could also devote

time to the practical questions of syllabuses, courses for pupils, and the demands of the classroom.[47]

Local Authorities and universities are already responding to this with specially tailored INSET courses,[48] for the message of the NFER survey is clear: language teachers *must* diversify. As far as Spanish is concerned we might set 1992 as our 'aim-by date': not only will it mark open frontiers but the Columbus quincentenary – Old and New Worlds together towards a new pattern of language education. The European Community has indeed stolen a march on us and declared 'the study of two languages to be essential'.[49] In terms of teacher provision, however, we might do well to avoid that other proposed European connection: the free movement of native speaker teachers, unused to and unprepared for our school and teaching conditions, who, we are told, will make good the current shortfall. We also need proper provision for the initial training of teachers. Why were there only 26 Hispanists in training in 1986–1987? (Teaching as a career is unattractive? Very few Hispanists applied to train? Too few UDE places available for Hispanists? Too few schools for them to do their teaching practice in? Any – but most likely a combination of all – of these may be the case.)

Materials and methods

Other information requested in the ATSP's survey had to do with the materials and tools needed for the job. Part of the infrastructure necessary for the planned development of Spanish concerns the availability of suitable courses, the genuine contact that can be made via school journey or exchange visits and the services of a Spanish language assistant.

Sadly, in 1984, only 3% of the schools surveyed had a full-time assistant, making it important to reiterate one of the Association's recommendations, 'that a system of central funding for foreign language assistants be established and that numbers be considerably increased'.[50] Sadly, too, more than half the schools reported no exchanges of visits. Here is much needed scope for development if we are to introduce pupils to the people, country, language and culture, to form links, create genuine interests and understanding – as well as ensure better grades at GCSE.

Whether teaching to GCSE, Graded Tests or A level, Spanish teachers are now much better served by publishers. Where the 1970s saw them tentatively buying the rights to a Swedish course here or there, we now have a very respectable range of courses and materials. Interestingly, even the 'top four' of 1984: *Calatrava, Adelante, Eso Es* and *¡Claro!* begin to look dated. We have indeed moved at an astonishing rate over the last 50 or so years: from the pioneers and *Principios* (1935), *Nos [pusimos] en camino* (1956) and later *Seguimos adelante*. It was then *¡Claro!*, that we got our *Pasaporte* and soon, *¡Vaya!*, after asking *¿Qué se dice?* and then practising *Cara a cara* we were to get the stamp of *¡Aprobado!*, *En directo desde España*.

Public performance

The authenticity implied in working *cara a cara* and *en directo* bring us to a consideration of aspects of public performance which represent the outcome of those years of work put in by the teachers (who at the same time are going on INSET courses, organising exchanges, making talk cards *and* finding the place on the tape . . .) and by their pupils.

It is a generally acknowledged fact that languages have probably been *the* area of the curriculum to benefit most from the introduction of the GCSE with its validation of the spoken language and its stress on credit for communication and, although, at this particular moment, the view is one of the 'teething' first years of operation, Spanish teachers, as much as others, welcome its advent wholeheartedly. This should prove a real springboard for an increase in teaching the language and to prove the point that an appropriate course and scheme of examination can work wonders, we only need to look at the pattern of entries over a series of decades:

Figure 2

1938	1965		1975		1985	
School Certificate	*GCE 'O'*	*CSE*	*GCE 'O'*	*CSE*	*GCE 'O'*	*CSE*
1,338	9,776	235	12,147	4,228	11,745	6,020

Examination of the figures shows:–

(1) natural and expected rise since immediate pre-war entry numbers;
(2) very low numbers for CSE in 1965, only the second year of a new-style examination, yet to prove its worth and respectability;
(3) having proved its worth, spectacular and ever-increasing numbers of CSE entries in 1975 and 1985;
(4) healthy overall rise over 20-year period in pupils being examined in Spanish at 16+ (10,011 to 17,765);
(5) increase, but also fluctuation, in figures for O level in the face of CSE uptake.

Overall, the picture shows the healthy growth state of Spanish; such growth was manifested essentially in the broader range of ability pupil for whom the CSE examination was deemed the most appropriate. An unequivocal stamp of approval for the egalitarian policy of offering the 'study of a foreign language to all, or nearly all, pupils'[51] (but beware of more 'Spanish for the least able'). We should be prepared to put money on the further increase in entries at 16+ in 1995.

Mention of 16+ makes one realise, however, that the GCSE is but one of a series of opportunities for pupils – and their teachers – to demonstrate performance. The greatest development of the 1980s has been in the Graded Tests area. Local initiatives, with teachers working on programmes appropriate to the stages, levels, and abilities of their pupils, have given an enormous impetus to successful, and properly rewarded, learning. We are lucky in having all the tools here for the job of teaching more Spanish to more pupils, in more schools in more parts of the country.

It is in the post-16 area, where entries for A level have been falling over the years (more at the bottom/younger end is very good, less at the upper end is not good), that a vigorous campaign for continuing (in addition, as is often the case to starting) Spanish is needed. New, much revised schemes of work and tests now characterise language study at this level: work done in the target language, less stress on literary studies, interpretation of authentic documents, investigation of areas of contemporary interest, such are the hallmarks of AS, Business Spanish and A levels. (There is also a very sound pragmatic reason for continued development at this level: we have to ensure the next generation of committed and well qualified Spanish teachers.)

Into the Nineties

Having looked back over a century of hard work, albeit accompanied by fluctuating fortunes, it is clear that there is a strong base, and the most positive of reasons, for moving forward into a future where we 'do away altogether with the idea that one and the same foreign language shall be learned by everybody'.[52]

The challenge of diversification is there for us to take on and it was indeed to this end that a whole section of the ATSP's 40th Anniversary Colloquium was devoted to the principles and examples of practice of giving Spanish its rightful place in the curriculum. The *Proceedings* of the Colloquium and a special issue of *Vida Hispánica*[53] represent a body of materials and arguments that will help teachers and other decision makers win the battle for a balanced language teaching programme and promote Spanish as being a 'realistic alternative'.[54]

The questions have been dealt with; we can now replace the question mark with the encouraging exclamation: Spanish – at last!

6

Community Languages: The Struggle for Survival

Farzana Turner

The extent of linguistic diversity in Britain

The presence of languages other than English in Britain is a fact now well documented. Research by Rosen and Burgess (1977)[1] showed the presence of 55 languages amongst 4,600 pupils in 28 schools in London. More recently, research carried out by the Linguistic Minorities Project[2] team not only demonstrated the range of languages present in five British cities but also gave a detailed picture of language use within some multilingual communities. One part of the research was a survey of languages spoken by school-age pupils in five Local Education Authorities (LEAs) – Bradford, Coventry, Haringey, Peterborough and Waltham Forest.

Information on numbers of pupils in schools speaking a language in addition to English in each LEA was provided in an aggregated form, so that, for example, Haringey was shown to have a bilingual pupil population of 30% and Bradford of 17.9%. No information was provided on individual schools where the bilingual population may have been virtually 100%.

The Linguistic Minorities Project survey also showed that the main languages

Figure 1

Proportions of bilingual pupils in five LEAs 1980 to 1981

LEA	No. of pupils surveyed	No. of bilingual pupils	% of bilingual pupils
Bradford	79,758	14,197	17.8
Haringey	24,140	7,383	30.7
Coventry	49,990	7,183	14.4
Peterborough	32,662	2,408	7.4
Waltham Forest	29,379	5,519	18.8

Figures taken from *The Other Languages of Britain*, LMP, 1985, London (RKP)

varied from area to area. In Bradford the main community languages were Panjabi and Urdu, whilst in Haringey the main languages found were Greek and Turkish. In addition to these, each of the LEAs had a number of other languages spoken by substantial numbers of pupils.

The range of languages present in particular areas and numbers of bilingual pupils has also been illustrated by local language surveys carried out by a number of LEAs. The recently completed NFER project on language provision for bilingual pupils[3] revealed that of the 88 LEAs in England and Wales responding, 32 had carried out language surveys. Unexpectedly, surveys in LEAs with relatively small numbers of ethnic minorities have also discovered a vast range of languages present. In Oxfordshire, for example, 66 different languages were found to be present among school-age pupils, although these represented only 4% of the total school population. However, in the city area of Oxford the percentage of bilingual pupils in schools was 13% and within a few schools the percentage of bilingual pupils was over 50%, reflecting the pattern elsewhere in the country.[4]

Figure 2

Distribution of bilingual pupils in Oxfordshire

	Oxford City	Banbury	County	Total
Number of bilingual pupils	1,565	335	770	2,670
Total number of school pupils	12,325	5,967	52,121	70,413
% bilingual pupils	13	6	1	4

There is a tendency to associate linguistic diversity with spoken skills only, but both the Linguistic Minorities Project and LEA surveys have shown that a substantial percentage of bilingual pupils also possess literacy skills in community languages. These skills cannot necessarily be quantified in terms of level of literacy, since most surveys have had to rely on responses given by pupils in schools. However, with the presence of many weekend language classes in city areas throughout Britain, where the main focus is the development of literacy skills, and the growing numbers of mainstream schools where community languages are offered as a subject within the curriculum, it would be reasonable to assume that many bilingual pupils in Britain do in fact possess a level of literacy in their first languages.

Among the languages present in various parts of Britain there are many European languages spoken by substantial numbers of bilingual pupils. In Peterborough, for example, the Linguistic Minorities Project found that 24% of all bilingual pupils had Italian as their mother tongue, and in Haringey Greek was the mother tongue of 34% of the bilingual pupils; however, language diversity in Britain has become synonymous with ethnic diversity and in particular with the presence of communities originating from the South Asian countries. This is illustrated in a response given by a Welsh LEA to the NFER survey referred to earlier. The LEA in question had approximately one-fifth of the primary school pupils speaking Welsh at home. A senior officer objected to the assumption in the NFER questionnaire that Welsh was a 'community language' since this term could be interpreted as relating to minority ethnic groups.

Similar responses have been made by headteachers responding to LEA surveys where information on linguistic diversity has been interpreted as information on the ethnicity of pupils in schools. One response to the LEA language survey from an Oxfordshire school where there were known to be six bilingual pupils with a European language was 'no immigrant pupils in this school'. Another school in the same authority refused to complete the questionnaire as it was felt that the information being sought was 'racist'. One needs to question whether it is this perception of languages in terms of ethnicity that may be at the root of the complex and often contradictory arguments presented when the position on community languages within the National Curriculum is discussed both at LEA and national level.

Educational response to linguistic diversity

Educational response to the presence of bilingual pupils has largely reflected the prevailing views by which minority groups could be integrated within British society. The initial reaction to the increasing number of immigrants in the 1960s, with very different life styles, cultures and religions, was to suggest assimilation into British society as a solution. The mechanism by which this was to be achieved was for the immigrant group to acquire English speedily. This was to be done with total disregard for the immigrants' own culture and languages. Many children were forbidden to use their mother tongues in schools, and indeed it was felt to be undesirable to have too many bilingual children in one school as they would adversely affect the quality of education provided in the school. A 1965 DES circular recommended that:

the proportion of immigrant children in any one school should not be unduly high.[5]

A limit of around 30% was thought to be appropriate by many, and in some areas where bilingual pupils exceeded this limit, the transportation by bus to other schools of bilingual pupils was used. The languages of ethnic minority communities were regarded solely as a problem, not just for themselves but also for their English speaking peers who were thought to be linguistically at risk in schools where bilingual pupils were at various stages in acquiring English.

The focus of attention was the language of the immigrant groups in that languages other than English were felt to be educationally undesirable; yet, at the same time, the very same pupils who were forbidden to use languages in which they were competent were attending lessons at secondary level to learn

French! Miller comments on how the languages of ethnic minorities were regarded in school:

> Whereas learning a foreign language and even one or two dead ones has always been the *sine qua non* of 'good' education and whereas a child who picks up fluent French and Italian, say, because her father has been posted abroad, is likely to be thought fortunate, at an advantage, even finished, a child with two or three non-European languages, in some of which he may be literate, could be regarded as literally languageless . . . [6]

It seems that the reduced status of particular languages was not due to their intrinsic worth but to how the languages were perceived in racial and cultural terms. The guiding philosophy of the 1960s and early 1970s was that the role of education was to provide cohesion and stability within society and that differences in cultures and languages should be actively discouraged within the educational system. The Robbins Committee Report in 1963 declared that one of the aims of education should be 'the transmission of a common culture'. This philosophy was not restricted to education alone. A view expressed as late as 1975 in the House of Lords was:

> It is the policy of the United Kingdom to seek and integrate migrant workers with the indigenous population rather than to further a multiracial society.

It is of interest that the educational philosophy and principles in Britain on the question of the desirability of a child-centred approach did not somehow extend to the languages and cultures of ethnic minorities; nor did a fundamental principle in the 1944 Education Act, which stated that education's role should be:

> To afford all pupils opportunities for education offering such variety of instruction and training as may be desirable in the view of their different ages, abilities and aptitudes.[7]

Clearly the 'abilities and aptitudes' within bilingual pupils' linguistic experience were to be completely ignored while a 'common culture' was being promoted.

The linguistic minority communities, however, ensured that their languages and cultures could survive by organising provision for the teaching of their languages outside school hours. Such provision has been in existence from the time when bilingual communities first became resident in Britain. The oldest voluntary language class recorded is described by the Commission for Racial Equality[8] as a Polish group established in Leicester in 1959. The same document also refers to two mosques where Urdu and Arabic have been taught since 1966.

By the mid-1970s there was a growing acceptance of the changing nature of British society and thinking in the DES began to reflect this. The 1977 Green Paper *Education in Schools* included the following statement:

> Our society is a multicultural and multiracial one and the curriculum should reflect a sympathetic understanding of different cultures and races which make up our society.[9]

This statement led to substantial developments in the area of multicultural education, and many LEAs appointed advisers and inspectors to support schools in developing an understanding of multicultural issues. The issue of linguistic diversity, however, was not addressed in a clear way despite the fact that the Bullock Report, *A Language for Life*,[10] just two years earlier, had made two very important statements in relation to the languages of bilingual pupils. The Report stated:

> The importance of bilingualism both in education and society in general has been increasingly recognised in Europe and the USA. We believe that its implications for Britain should receive equally serious study. When bilingualism in Britain is described it is seldom done with reference to the inner-city immigrant population, yet over half the immigrant pupils in our schools have a mother tongue which is not English and in some schools this means over 75% of the total number on roll ... these children are genuine bilinguals, but this fact is often ignored or unrecognised by the school. Their bilingualism is of great importance to the children and their families and to society as a whole. In a linguistically conscious nation in a modern world we should see it as an asset ...

Bullock continues:

> No child should be expected to cast off the language and the culture of the home as he crosses the school threshold nor to live and act as though school and home represent two totally separate and different cultures which have to be kept firmly apart.

Neither the statements in the Bullock Report nor the rapid development in the area of multicultural and multiethnic education had any real effect on the position of community languages within education. Although English language support was being provided during the 1970s, usually by teachers of English as a Second Language (ESL) on a peripatetic basis, and some notice was being taken of pupils' cultures within schools, no acknowledgement was made of the first language of bilingual pupils, other than continuing to perceive them as a problem. First, and by now second generation ethnic minority pupils' mother tongues remained within their home and within their local community. The real catalyst in bringing issues related to language diversity in Britain to the forefront of educational debate has been the European Commission Directive of 1977. Article Three of the Directive stated:

> Member States shall in accordance with their national circumstances and legal systems and in cooperation with states of origin take appropriate measures to promote in accordance with normal education teaching of the mother tongue and culture of the country of origin for the children referred to in Article One.[11]

Article One in fact referred to Member States. However, within the context of Britain the then Secretary of State, Mark Carlisle, declared that it was the DES's intention to apply the Directive without regard to the country of origin of the children. Four years subsequent to notification in July 1981, all Member States were required to have taken appropriate measures to comply with the Directive. As the original wording of the Directive as presented in the draft version (1976) had been amended by 1977 to include 'in accordance with their national and legal system', the intention of the Directive was open to interpretation. The DES saw its obligation as no more than furthering research into the educational benefits of bilingualism. In July 1981 the DES set out its response to the European Commission Directive:

> For its part the DES is sponsoring research related to the provision and educational implications of mother tongue teaching as well as taking a close interest in European Commission sponsored initiatives in this country.[12]

The same circular also saw it as the responsibility of LEAs to explore ways in which mother tongue teaching could be provided either in the mainstream curriculum or outside school hours.

Such an interpretation in Britain was clearly a reflection of a lack of commitment to supporting bilingual pupils' mother tongue skills. It was also a reflection of a continuing belief that the first languages of bilingual pupils were not desirable and that any provision for mother tongue teaching within LEAs should not be encouraged. The Home Affairs Select Committee Report of 1981 declared that the UK was not under any legal obligation to provide mother tongue teaching particularly to those who were not from Member States. The Report also stated that:

> We are not convinced either that the Local Education Authority is under any obligation to provide mother tongue teaching or that it is necessarily in the general interest that they should do so.[13]

Yet the Report supported the inclusion of non-European languages in the modern languages curriculum. It also suggested that details of examinations at O and A levels in the mother tongues of bilingual pupils should be published in the annual statistics of the Department. Within such an approach there were clear implications for the status that would be attached to bilingual pupils' languages. The neglect of the mother tongue at the primary level meant that these languages were to be regarded as unimportant in the context of education by both bilingual parents and children. On the one hand pupils were to be discouraged from developing their mother tongues during the early years, and on the other, the same languages were offered at secondary level. Inevitably the take-up of community languages in secondary schools was low. There was also an underlying assumption that community languages were only relevant to bilingual pupils; whereas these languages could be taught in secondary schools, they were not to be given the genuine status of modern languages, to allow Urdu or Greek possibly to be taught in place of, say, French to all children.

Such a philosophy was to some extent reflected in the recommendations of the Swann Report, *Education for All*.[14] Whilst Swann accepted the importance of the child's mother tongue during the early stages of acquiring English and for providing confidence in adjusting to the school environment, the Report did not see it as the responsibility of primary schools to provide continued support for pupils' mother tongues. However, it was suggested that community languages should be offered alongside the modern languages curriculum at secondary level to all pupils. The Report argued that there should not be an artificial distinction between ethnic minority community languages and modern languages. Section 3.19 stated:

> The educational value to an individual of learning a language other than his own is an indisputable component of a full and balanced education. However, the pre-eminence of French and German as the languages offered by schools, while perhaps originally having been based on sound educational reasons, seems in today's interdependent world and within our own multibilingual environment, somewhat harder to explain and defend. Within the context of 'Education for All' we believe it to be entirely right for a white English speaking pupil to study an ethnic minority community language as a valid and integral part of his education.

In relation to bilingual pupils studying their own languages at secondary level the Report went on to say:

> We believe it is only reasonable to expect that he should be able to study for a qualification in a language in which he already has some facility.

There were important statements indicating the DES position on the place of community languages within the secondary curriculum. Swann also recommended that the modern languages adviser/inspector should be responsible for community languages in LEAs, once again reinforcing the place of community languages within modern languages.

The lack of any recommendation supporting the development of mother tongue teaching in a cohesive way within primary schools was disappointing. The Report suggested that the responsibility for the teaching of community languages prior to any provision at secondary level should be with ethnic minority communities, though the LEA should make an effort to provide support for resources, accommodation and in-service training for voluntary teachers. Such a recommendation did not fit in with the overall philosophy within *Education for All*. In an attempt to emphasise the importance for all children to develop an understanding of the culturally and ethnically diverse nature of British society, the Report failed to address the area of continuity in bilingual pupils' language learning as part of their education.

Despite the very clear support within the Swann Report for community languages as part of the modern languages curriculum at secondary level, their position was once again placed in jeopardy when they were treated as a separate issue in the *Foreign Languages in the School Curriculum (FLISC)* discussion document. This led to a great deal of speculation during the past three years as to whether community languages would ever be placed within the mainstream curriculum. The *FLISC* document stated:

> The place such community languages should take in the school curriculum is an important and complex question which in our view merits more detailed consideration

than was possible in the consultations which preceded this statement. We intend therefore to publish a consultative document on this issue in due course.[15]

Such a consultative document, even though there were pressures from various organisations (such as the National Council for Mother Tongue Teaching) for its publication, was never published. Instead, two years later, community languages were again excluded from the DES Statement of Policy, *Modern Languages in the School Curriculum (MLISC)*[16] other than regarding their position as outside the concerns of the policy statement. The document declared that 'We intend to consult separately on this issue in due course'. This exclusion of community languages and the uncertainty as to whether a separate consultation paper would ever appear, resulted in many LEAs, where provision for community languages had been made within the curriculum, wondering if it would be possible to continue this in the future within the National Curriculum. Others who were about to embark on provision in schools were reluctant to move further until final decisions had been made as to which languages would be included as part of the National Curriculum. However, it is important to look at the rationale that was already stated for the inclusion of a modern language among the foundation subjects and to relate this to community languages. It is worth exploring ways in which community languages already fit into the arguments for the teaching of modern languages in the curriculum. Separate consultations, statements, or even lists of languages, are perhaps not necessary.

LEA provision for the teaching of community languages

LEAs' provision to meet the needs of bilingual pupils has historically been in terms of English language support. Over the years this has taken many forms. In some LEAs in the 1960s language centres were set up where pupils, instead of attending mainstream school, would attend a language centre for, in some cases, up to two years. Here English would be taught to them, but little account was taken of the curriculum of mainstream schools. The pupils would, after attending the centre, enter the local school and were expected to function as native speakers of English. This withdrawal of pupils did not in fact have the effect it was intended to have. In reality it was found that bilingual pupils did not achieve as well as their monolingual peers and in many cases performed very poorly at examination level. In other LEAs English language support was provided within school-based language units with pupils being withdrawn from their classes for extra English teaching. Once again the language taught was unrelated to the curriculum, and these pupils also performed poorly in class. However, over the past few years there has been a move away from ESL being taught on a withdrawal basis. Increasingly ESL teachers are working alongside mainstream teachers and teaching within the classroom, so that the language being taught is relevant and related to the curriculum.

As far as support for pupils' mother tongues was concerned, very little provision was made until the beginning of the 1980s. As already mentioned, the

European Commission Directive was a major catalyst in this development. Another factor that led to provision for mother tongue and community language teaching being made in schools was the use of Section 11 funds (Local Government Act, 1966).

This fund came into existence in response to an increasing ethnic minority population in the 1960s. It was made available to local authorities for the employment of staff in areas where there were substantial numbers of immigrants whose language and culture differed from those of the rest of the community. Section 11 was intended to meet the specific needs of immigrants and their descendants from Commonwealth countries. The funds, which covered 75% of staff salaries, were to be in addition to any provision that would normally be made within the authority. Many authorities where Section 11 funds were being used for ESL provision also made use of these funds to provide teachers of community languages. This has continued to be the pattern, and 88% of all posts concerned with mother tongue teaching and community languages are funded by Section 11.[17]

This use of Section 11 funds for community languages provision rather than funding from LEAs' mainstream funds, is an indication of community languages being perceived as meeting the additional needs of ethnic minority pupils and not an extension of the range of languages offered within the modern languages curriculum. For European languages which are the mother tongues of European bilingual pupils, additional resources are provided in many cases through their European consulates. The use of additional funding for community languages provision in conjunction with the lack of commitment or direction from the DES (until March 1989) on the provision of community languages in the curriculum, has led to *ad hoc* provision for community language teaching around the country. To date there is no LEA with a cohesive policy in relation to community language teaching.

Some LEAs have a policy of supporting weekend supplementary schools only. Teachers' salaries are paid, and school premises are made available free of charge. There is also some in-service training organised for the teachers, and usually fairly limited funds are provided for teaching and learning resources. It remains to be seen how far the recommendations of the Swann Report and the current practice of many LEAs of making school premises available free of charge will be affected by the Education Reform Act (1988) where under Local Management of Schools the governing bodies of the school will be responsible for their funds in respect of teachers' salaries, premises and running costs.

A number of LEAs have made provision for the teaching of community languages within mainstream schools. Birmingham, for example, has a team of seventeen community language teachers at secondary level. Eighteen secondary schools offer a community language within the curriculum, and 2,134 pupils studied one of the community languages offered in schools in the year 1987–1988. Approximately 250 pupils passed an external 16+ examination, and fourteen pupils passed A level in a community language in 1988. In addition to this provision, supplementary language classes are also supported through the use of Inner City Partnership Funds. It is estimated that some 5,000 pupils are involved in attending these classes.[18]

In Oxfordshire there are seven secondary schools (middle and upper) where community languages are taught within the curriculum. In some cases in middle schools, where the timetables are less flexible, pupils opt out of particular lessons to attend community language classes. Six supplementary schools are supported where teachers' salaries are paid and in-service training is offered. There is also substantial provision at primary level, where primary schools have support from peripatetic bilingual teachers working with bilingual pupils within mainstream classes.

Of the 88 LEAs in England and Wales which responded to the NFER survey referred to earlier, 82% were making some additional provision for bilingual pupils. Of these, 36 were making specific provision for support of pupils' mother tongues or for the teaching of community languages. Over 640 schools, distributed over a third of all LEAs, were making provision within the curriculum for community languages. This is a substantial increase on the picture revealed from the survey of mother tongue provision in LEAs carried out by Townsend in 1971, where only 3% of the LEAs in the country were found to make provision for community language teaching.

The gradual and increasing amount of support for the teaching of community languages in many LEAs around the country, albeit in the main funded from external sources, has resulted in community languages being taught in the curriculum in many British schools. However, the take-up for these languages by white monolingual pupils is poor since they continue to be perceived as only relevant to ethnic minority pupils and their status remains low. In an effort to raise the status of community languages and to move away from the notion of only European languages being important (usually only French and German), some schools have taken the initiative of including non-European languages as part of language awareness programmes. In such programmes, all pupils are able to experience a non-European language. In some cases this takes the form of one or two 'taster' sessions, and in others this element is more substantial. Banbury School in Oxfordshire, for example, with relatively few bilingual pupils, has included Urdu as one of the languages in a carousel of languages studied by all pupils for one hour per week for a term.

The increase in the teaching of community languages in schools and the efforts being made in some schools to involve all pupils in learning such a language demonstrate positive moves towards the acceptance that Britain is not just multicultural and multiethnic, but also multilingual. The multilingual nature of British society is referred to by the Kingman Committee's report. This recommends that 'it should be the duty of all teachers to instil in their pupils a civilised respect for other languages'.[19] The Cox Report sees the presence of bilingual children as an asset to Britain's economy, stating that:

> the presence of large numbers of bilingual and biliterate children in the community should be seen as an enormous resource which ought to become more, not less, important in the British economy in the next few years.[20]

It was therefore quite incomprehensible that, as is made clear in the DES policy statement on the teaching of modern languages on the school curriculum, community languages were not seen to have a proper role to play. That has now changed.

Community languages in the National Curriculum

It was good news when the Secretary of State indicated that a list of languages to be taught in schools within the National Curriculum would be specified. The debate to date has focussed on arguments for the inclusion of such languages as a separate issue and in relation to provision being made for bilingual pupils to study their languages within the curriculum. Very little effort has been made to explore ways in which the arguments put forward for the inclusion of a modern foreign language in the National Curriculum (which has usually been interpreted as a European language) apply equally to community languages and to make it clear that these languages are relevant to all pupils.

It could almost be argued that as the discussion documents on *Foreign Languages in the School Curriculum* were concerned with 'foreign languages' and clearly languages such as Panjabi, spoken by thousands of people in Britain, are not foreign, there should be a separate consultation document for community languages. However, the exclusion of such languages from the document entitled *Modern Languages in the School Curriculum*[21] is more difficult to understand and accept. By any definition, community languages *are* modern languages and therefore could justifiably claim a place in the document and in the National Curriculum. It is essential that there is a move away from the perception of some languages as being 'modern' and others as being the languages of ethnic minorities living in Britain. Without this perception, the distinction between modern and community languages would not exist.

It is of interest that the Statement of Policy uses three terms, 'modern languages', 'foreign languages' and 'modern foreign languages', to describe languages other than English and the Classics in the curriculum. This vagueness of terminology led to uncertainty as to what criteria would be used to define the languages to be included as a Foundation Subject in the National Curriculum. Any criteria that excluded ethnic minority languages would clearly have to take into account any legal implications in relation to discrimination under the Race Relations Act of 1976. The rationale in the policy statement for teaching a 'modern foreign language' to all pupils falls into two categories – educational and commercial. The document, in relation to education benefits, states that:

> Learning a foreign language brings educational benefits beyond the attainments of practical skills, important as they are. It offers insights into the nature of language and language learning.

It goes on to say:

> It can promote a disciplined and active approach to learning and the satisfaction of gaining competence and understanding which are both rewarding and useful.[22]

These statements surely apply to any new language that a pupil may study; these benefits would equally be the outcome of studying either German or Gujarati. The document also, on a number of occasions, refers to the use that could be made of the skills in a modern language 'by people at work or in their personal lives at home and abroad'. Under this argument there would be certain advantages in learning one of the languages spoken in Britain. It would allow for an opportunity to use such languages in both the context of this country and in countries where those languages are spoken as national languages.

In acknowledging the presence of community languages the document refers to 'a climate of awareness of languages' and to the fact that this 'opens up interesting and challenging opportunities for language learning'. The effect of negative attitudes towards learning languages is referred to:

> Negative attitudes to learning languages are self-perpetuating; if young people are not encouraged to see foreign language skills as an asset, they are unlikely to pursue their study to a point where it will be worthwhile or, later on, to encourage their own children to do so.[23]

Young people do not always distinguish between the varied status of the languages in Britain. It may be that it is the general negative attitude towards the languages of ethnic minorities that has led to the poor take-up of languages by young people in Britain. Unless all languages are treated equally there may continue to be uncertainties in people's minds as to the value of learning a language other than their own.

The importance of studying a foreign language for commercial purposes and for improving our national capability is strongly stated throughout the policy statement. The document argues that the study of a foreign language can help to serve the needs of the country. It states that the country:

> can benefit economically and culturally. Opportunities will be opened up in trade, tourism, international relations, science and other fields.[24]

This statement is in relation to 'Britain's effectiveness as a member of the European Community'. It is likely that here the learning of European languages was envisaged. However, paragraph 3 clearly refers to the importance of learning both European and other languages for commercial purposes. It states:

> Compared with major trading nations, ours has a damagingly small proportion of people who understand and speak a modern foreign language.[25]

It goes on to argue that although English can be used for trade in places such as North America and the Commonwealth where English has a currency, 'a complete reliance on it narrows opportunities in business and other respects.' The policy statement has declared that it is undesirable to perpetuate the dominance of the teaching of French in schools and that there is a need to diversify the modern languages taught. The document advocates that:

> Local Education Authorities and schools should ensure that a reasonable proportion of their pupils of all abilities study a language other than French as their first foreign language.[26]

It is suggested that to secure diversification in the first foreign languages studied, larger schools where French is available, should offer two alternative first foreign languages, and smaller schools should explore the possibility of teaching another language in place of French, with French as a second foreign language. Unfortunately it was considered that diversification should be limited to certain European languages. The arguments to justify this were that there would be 'very little teaching capacity in these languages and it is unlikely to be a cost-effective use of resources to provide them within schools for pupils of compulsory school age'.[27]

Not many people arguing for community languages to be taught in the curriculum would suggest that on commercial grounds every school or even a quarter of the schools in the country should teach a community language as a first foreign language to all the pupils. Quite clearly this would not be appropriate in a European county where commercial and social links with other European countries are well-established and are likely to be greater beyond 1992. However, not to have these languages as a first language in schools where parents are supportive and pupils wish to study them, for whatever purposes, would mean both restricting choice for monolingual pupils and giving strong messages to ethnic minority pupils that their languages do not have the status of being included within the National Curriculum.

Where next?

Government policies in relation to the education of ethnic minority groups seem to have shifted from a policy of national cohesion (to the detriment of the heritage culture of minority groups) to supporting ethnic and cultural diversity and ensuring that all pupils are aware of the multicultural nature of present-day British society. The issue of the languages of ethnic minorities has not really been resolved and continues to be debated. The opportunity for pupils to study any modern language as a Foundation Subject in the National Curriculum seems to have become entangled with this debate. There is no reason why there should be restrictions on the choice of languages that can be taught as a first foreign language in a school irrespective of whether the school has an ethnic minority population.

It is highly unlikely that, now that community languages are included in the National Curriculum, there will be a sudden explosion around the country of large numbers of schools teaching community languages as first foreign languages. However, to specify a list of European languages only would have had long-term repercussions on the position and status of ethnic minority communities in Britain. It would also have been contradictory to the many recommendations that have been made by the DES and HMI which have been in favour of the inclusion of community languages in the multilingual curriculum.

As stated earlier, as well as ethnic minority bilingual pupils, there are many bilingual pupils in Britain originating from European countries. Since a list of

European languages has been specified, such pupils will have an opportunity to study their home language within the National Curriculum. Ethnic minority children will now have such an opportunity in schools *wishing to* offer their languages.

The survival of community languages is dependent on the following four factors:

(a) Ethnic minority languages being adequately recognised, protected and maintained for the original speakers of those languages through a variety of strategies within the mainstream curriculum.

(b) Children seeing community languages as valuable and being encouraged to learn them. It is the use of minority languages by non-native speakers that will ensure their survival in Britain.

(c) Community language teachers being funded from mainstream funds (and not Section 11 funds, which results in the perception that community language teaching is solely to meet the additional needs of ethnic minority pupils). Mainstream funding will ensure that any decision to teach a community language is one that is concerned with the extension of the modern language curriculum.

(d) Teacher training and higher education institutions offering courses which will increase the supply of trained teachers to teach community languages in schools.

All these will follow naturally if community languages find a proper place in the National Curriculum. As this book was going to press it was announced, as David Phillips describes in the Introduction, that non-EC languages, including the major community languages, can be taught alongside the 'working languages of the European Community'. Their inclusion in the National Curriculum is dependent upon an EC language being offered as an alternative. While this arrangement is a step forward, many feel that it falls far short of according community languages the status they deserve.

However, there are others who believe that the two schedules are appropriate in the context of the UK. The arguments used are that if a European language was not offered in every school, then in some areas where there are large numbers of ethnic minority bilingual pupils *only* a community language would be offered. This, post-1992, might add to the many disadvantages such pupils already have within our education system; not allowing a choice for those who wish to learn a European language might result in a restriction of career opportunities in the future. The debate on this issue will continue, and we need to explore both the positive and the negative implications of the inclusion of community languages in the form that has been agreed.

Welsh within the National Curriculum

Geraint Wyn Jones

Historical background

The Welsh language was the only vehicle of communication in use in Wales for centuries. For the medieval storyteller, poet and cleric, it was the only available medium of expression. The situation was little changed at the outset of the nineteenth century when 'the religious vocabulary of the Welsh language [had] been enlarged, strengthened and rendered capable of expressing every shade of idea, and the great mass of the poorer classes [had] been trained from childhood to its use'.[1] The English language only began to make serious inroads in education with the advent of the British (1808) and National (1811) schools. Indeed, it was as a result of a National schools report that the need to find 'the means afforded to the labouring classes of acquiring a knowledge of the English language'[2] was first voiced as a priority in Welsh-speaking Wales.

Once adopted, this objective became the yardstick by which all future educational endeavours would be measured – Welsh language activity being either derided or completely ignored. The Revised Code of 1862, which decreed that teachers would henceforth be paid according to their pupils' command of English, opportunely endorsed the view. It was further enhanced by Britain's emerging imperial role, where political power and linguistic dominance were inextricably intertwined. It is this climate of opinion that explains the view held by the 'Commissioners of Inquiry' (1847) that:

> The Welsh language is a vast drawback to Wales, and a manifold barrier to the moral progress and commercial prosperity of the people. It dissevers the people from intercourse which would greatly advance their civilisation, and bars the access of improving knowledge to their minds.[3]

This 'official' view was quickly embraced by the Welsh establishment itself, with prominent members such as the Reverend D J Davies of Emmanuel College, Cambridge,[4] and the Reverend Kilsby-Jones fervently advocating the liberation of 'the now poor, despised monoglot Welshman from his mountain prison and [opening] before him the four quarters of the globe'.[5] Such a view was the product of, and reinforced by, a concurrence of factors. When the 1870 Education Act was implemented, for example, the only institutional educational models available were the National and British schools. The same was true when the university colleges of Wales were established, from 1872 onwards, on the lines of the University of London and other provincial university colleges. These Welsh institutions were therefore run, from the outset, on English lines, by products of the English education system. It is hardly surprising therefore that when the Cross Commission allowed Welsh to be taught concurrently with English in schools or when such pioneering educators as Dan Isaac Davies, and later O M Edwards, exhorted them to make greater use of Welsh within their schools, Welsh teachers were somewhat reluctant to face the linguistic challenges involved.

The nineteenth and twentieth centuries witnessed many other developments that were to condition the linguistic attitudes of the Welsh. Wales was brought closer to England by means of canal, road and rail links. There were also widespread industrial developments, mostly financed by English entrepreneurs, and such undertakings inevitably served to link prosperity with anglicisation and Welshness with poverty in the popular mind. Such attitudes were later reinforced by significant developments in popular culture (the daily newspaper, the cinema), the field of technology (the telephone, broadcasting, Information Technology), by a decline in religious observance, and important social changes (emigration, immigration, tourism, urbanisation).

The challenges such changes brought in their wake were not initially of unmanageable proportions. Had not the educational response been so uncoordinated, their linguistic influence would probably have been contained. Such fragmentation can at times be very clearly seen. In 1897, for example, the Rhondda appointed designated Welsh teachers to instruct their pupil teachers, over half of whom opted to study Welsh rather than French. During the same period there was also considerable linguistic activity in Cardiff and parts of South-East Wales. Meanwhile, elsewhere in Wales the Government's new, permissive attitude towards Welsh was largely being ignored.

A more typical attitude towards Welsh is mirrored in the educational codes. The first Welsh code of 1907 bitterly complains that 'Welsh is often taught in English, though to the pupil the vehicle of instruction is the language less perfectly known . . .', whilst the report of 1915 notes that there were 22 schools without a single Welsh book in their libraries at the time. In 1919 there were still schools where Welsh did not figure in the daily curriculum, and the situation had hardly improved when the seminal report *Welsh in Education and Life* was published in 1927. This lukewarm and at times negative attitude amongst Welsh educational providers (though running contrary to Welsh public opinion surveys),[6] persisted into the second half of the twentieth century and has only recently undergone significant change.

Recent developments

The establishment of the first 'designated' Welsh primary school (*Ysgol Gymraeg*) at Aberystwyth in 1939, although a privately funded establishment, marked the beginning of institutional educational change in Wales. Its importance lies in the fact that it was a ready model when such schools were later established within the public sector. The first such publicly funded institution opened its doors at Llanelli in 1944; to date there are 67 primary *Ysgolion Cymraeg*. It was almost inevitable that such developments would create a demand for secondary Welsh-medium education, culminating in the establishment of the first designated Welsh secondary school at Rhyl in 1956. Currently there are eighteen such schools within the national system. These 'designated' schools (although mostly founded in the anglicised areas of Wales) have in turn influenced educational provision in 'natural' Welsh-speaking areas and have been a key factor in promoting bilingual education throughout Wales. In 1987 there were 463 primary schools where Welsh was either 'the sole or main medium of instruction or containing classes where some of the teaching occurred through the medium of Welsh'.[7] At the secondary level (using similar criteria) the figure was 53.

Such activity (within the statutory provision) triggered other developments both at the further/higher and nursery ends of the spectrum. Convinced that an early start yielded better second language results, Welsh nursery schools (*Ysgolion Meithrin*) began to emerge, in the early 1960s, specifically to take advantage of the fact. These, initially, were voluntary concerns, receiving financial assistance only after a charitable trust had been set up in 1963 expressly to promote their activity. In 1971, a national committee was established to oversee and coordinate developments; by today (1989) the movement has a total number of 580 groups.[8]

Developments in higher education have been mainly centred on the university colleges of Aberystwyth and Bangor, these having been designated as centres of Welsh medium teaching by the University of Wales. In the academic year 1987–1988, for example, 251 students studied some part of their course through the medium of Welsh at Aberystwyth and 238 at Bangor (these figures do not include students exclusively studying the Welsh language and its literature).[9] During the same period, 375 students followed comparable studies at the Normal College of Education, Bangor, and at Trinity College, Carmarthen. It must be noted, however, that the developments that have occurred have been mainly in the arts; developments in the sciences to date (owing in part to a lack of Welsh-speaking expertise in specialised fields, and in part to the limited numbers involved) being much more hesitant and slow. The situation is at present being appraised (at further education level) by a Welsh Office-funded research project, centred at Llangefni, whilst a similar study (looking at University provision) is currently under way at University College, Bangor.

The developments outlined above are anything but uniform. All Gwynedd schools, for example, at present provide some form of bilingual education, whereas in contrast, Gwent has only a handful of Welsh units within its ordinary schools. Gwent too has only recently begun to address the issue of secondary Welsh medium education with the establishment, in 1987, of its first bilingual secondary school. This disparity of provision is, as one would expect, mirrored in the variety of language policies currently operated by Welsh LEAs. Gwynedd, for example, formulated a comprehensive bilingual policy at its inception in 1975 and this was recently modified to meet changing social and linguistic needs.[10] Gwent on the other hand has no formal language policy[11] and seems to have adopted a largely pragmatic approach to the bilingual challenge. The policies of other counties are to be found somewhere along a range of provision between the two extremes.

Such fragmentation is in part due to the uneven spread of Welsh speakers throughout the population. A county with a recorded Welsh-speaking population of only 2.5% will almost certainly view bilingual education differently from one with the highest density of Welsh speakers in Wales.[12] But there are other equally valid contributory factors such as traditional long-established links with the Welsh heartland, the proximity to Welsh-speaking areas, and the strength of parental demand for a 'balanced' bilingual education.

The National Curriculum: Welsh Working Group Interim Report, November 1988

The uneven provision would seem to have affected the decision to include Welsh (in Wales) within the National Curriculum. Successive Government reports have noted significant variations in the time allocated to Welsh within the schools and the unacceptable and diverse interpretations of such other apposite factors as the starting age, linguistic progression, teaching approach, methodology, language use, language contact, attitude, etc.[13] Such disparities could not have been attractive to a Government in search of educational uniformity and efficiency. The National Curriculum will, therefore, attempt to ensure that Welsh can, for the first time, 'be a compulsory subject from infant through to school leaving age'[14] giving it in future unequivocal Government status and support.

The Education Reform Act (1988) established a National Curriculum in England and Wales composed of foundation and core subjects. The core subjects in all schools will be: mathematics, science, and English; in 'Welsh-speaking' schools Welsh will also be included in the core. Such schools are defined as those where more than one half of either religious education, history, music, geography, technology, art and physical education are taught (wholly or partly) in Welsh. Welsh will be a foundation subject in the remaining Welsh schools.

A supplementary guidance document provides some intimation of the weighting of such 'foundation' courses.[15] 'The [working] group could assume that on average 20% of total curriculum time' would be available for Welsh in Welsh-speaking schools, the percentage being 'between 10% and 12.5%' in ordinary schools. The definition in fact does little more than mirror current practice (in the majority of Welsh schools), a fact which could not but have influenced the summary conclusions of the Interim Report. For, although the group was instructed not to 'consider itself bound rigidly by the distinction between core and other foundation subjects', it was inevitable that the 'official' interpretation (in which, rather significantly, the language is referred to throughout as a 'subject') should constrain their deliberations, and considerably restrict their options. *De facto*, the daunting task presented to them was to marry their ideals to the harsh realities of the existing provision.

Another influential factor appears to have been the fact that a modern language will also be a foundation subject within the National Curriculum. It only attains that distinction, however, at the secondary level. Welsh, on the other hand, will be taught both at the primary and secondary level, thus enabling Welsh teachers to formulate more ambitious plans than their modern language colleagues. This extended contact period must have been one of the factors that induced the working group to think in second language terms. Welsh will therefore be taught 'Not as a foreign language but as an alternative natural medium of communication in Wales'.[16]

This distinction is all-important and has far-reaching consequences and implications for any language learning programme. A second 'alternative . . . medium of communication' implies that there will be no essential difference in use between the first and second acquired tongue. It further suggests that the developmental programmes needed both by the native speaker and the second language learner will in essence be the same. There would naturally, at times, be a difference in emphasis and, at others, a difference in pace, but the ultimate objectives would essentially be the same, regardless of linguistic background.

Such a second language definition is certainly in accord with the views of the English working group. In its deliberations on the attainments of Welsh children studying English as their second tongue it states that:

> The Programmes of Study in English for the 8 to 11 age group will need *modification* to accommodate the needs of Welsh First Language pupils whose first formal teaching in and through English has been delayed until the age of 7. Such modification need only be *slight* . . . We assume that the Secondary Examinations and Assessment Council . . . will develop assessment processes which reflect the fact that there are *similar developmental stages*.[17]

The objectives reinforce an underlying belief in the unity of the language learning process, a second language being regarded as second merely in terms of time. It is in fact another main language with which a person can come to terms with the world.

On decreeing Welsh to be 'an alternative . . . medium of communication' one would have expected the Welsh group also to accept the concomitant view that 'there is a unity of process that characterises all language acquisition, whether first or second language and [that] . . . this unity of process reflects the use of similar strategies of language acquisition'.[18] The logical consequence would then have been for it to favour a single language programme (slightly modified for some) to attain that goal. The wide variation of linguistic and teaching situations in Wales, however, seems to have outweighed such pedagogical considerations, hence the Report prescribes two distinct programmes, one for the first language, another for the second.

In order successfully to acquire a second tongue, certain minimum requirements (such as extended contacts with the language within a variety of meaningful contexts) would seem to have to be met.[19] Such conditions, however, are prominent only within the first language part of the Report. Nowhere are they stipulated as the prerequisites of second language success. The indeterminate nature of the second language aims (and the multiplicity of terms used to denote them) would also seem to be at variance with the original objectives set. In some sections the Report expects 'the great majority of [the] second language pupils [to] achieve a *reasonable* degree of fluency in Welsh',[20] at other times a '*substantial* degree of fluency'[21] is foreseen, while in the profile components the learner is expected to be able to 'persuade', 'theorise', and 'convey and seek information'. Whilst it is difficult to reconcile the more modest of these targets with customary second language proficiency, the more ambitious would seem to be impossible to attain, at least under the teaching conditions imposed.

There seems therefore to be an inherent contradiction within the Welsh Report. The working group, on the one hand, espouse second language ideals whilst at the same time limiting the conditions necessary to attain them to the first language field. Such inconsistencies can be seen even within the second language section of the Report. Whereas the preamble would appear to advocate vibrant, exploratory language learning ('presenting Welsh by means of lively, varied and interesting activities in a happy and relaxed atmosphere')[22], the 'Guidance about the targets' suggests a somewhat rigid and more mechanical approach: so much so that it is not unfair to argue that the creation of a separate second language programme (as presently constituted) is an arrangement that would seem to negate and nullify the very objectives it was created to serve.

The apparent mismatch can be accounted for in many ways. It has long been the custom in Wales to discuss Welsh language teaching in first and second language terms, the designations often having little regard to actual teaching conditions. A more realistic analysis would reveal the existence of at least three definable teaching situations in Welsh schools.

(1) In the first, the contact time is brief, and 'language learning' the primary objective, 'language using' being a development rarely considered. Such conditions normally obtain in the 'foreign language' field.

(2) In the second, the language is used increasingly as a learning tool (an alternative means of expression), with the learner constantly forging links with new experiences in his second tongue.

(3) The third is the first language situation which (as one would expect) has much in common with the conditions described immediately above.

Viewed in this way, the link between appropriate learning conditions and second language success becomes abundantly clear. It is equally apparent that limitations can stifle such aspirations, preventing the learning from moving beyond the language structure itself. With a time allocation of 10% to 12.5% there is little hope that anything else can be done.

That the Report should circumvent this crucial issue has more to do with emotional ties than with educational theory. The 'foreign language' tag understandably provokes strong reactions in Wales. It is ignominious to Welsh speakers that their language should be regarded as foreign within its own domain. Context analysis, however, reveals that second language programmes have only operated hitherto within 'natural' and 'designated' Welsh schools, other schools in reality operating mostly under 'foreign language' conditions. The National Curriculum would, therefore, seem to present a rare opportunity (under appropriate conditions) to expand the provision of a truly bilingual education throughout the schools of Wales.

The fear that such an ambitious plan might be counter-productive is understandable. Schools currently enjoying a modicum of success (in teaching Welsh) might well be driven to despair. On the other hand, viewed positively, a single comprehensive, flexibly structured programme could prove an invigorating linguistic challenge, enabling *all* learners to enjoy a measure of success. It would both unify the language learning process and mirror the range of proficiency encountered within all linguistic groups. But, more importantly, it would free teachers from the shackles of chronologically orientated attainment-targets to focus on meeting individual linguistic needs.

Embracing the 'unity of process' standpoint would have made bilingualism once more a central issue in Wales. Regarded as a 'subject' (taught as a language rather than used as a medium), the Welsh language obviously needs no more time allocated to it than any other area of the curriculum. But if it is to coexist with English on equal terms, the same operating conditions for both languages should apply. By opting for two distinct language programmes, the Working Group adroitly side-stepped the fundamental linguistic problem facing Wales today, choosing prudently instead to endorse the *status quo*.

By shielding the learner from the target community the binary approach also impedes any acculturisation that is likely to occur. One would have therefore expected the issue to be discussed at some length within the Welsh language report. Scant attention, however, is given to this crucial learning aspect, the problem of moving pupils 'from one group to another', for example, being postponed until the final report. The ways in which the Welsh television channel (S.4C.), the Welsh radio station (*Radio Cymru*), new electronic communication and information channels, exchange visits between Welsh and less Welsh areas, and the recently-founded adult learner/native speaker societies could provide much greater language contact are at best regarded as peripheral, and at worst completely ignored. No consideration is given to the place of intervention programmes (such as those of guided play) in linguistic schemes, and no reference made to community education, generally regarded as a vital component if the learner is ever to use the language *purposefully* outside the classroom walls.

The Report, however, does make one important linguistic stand. The supplementary guidance had argued that 'knowledge about language' should be taught quite independently of the four main language skills. The Welsh group, on the other hand, saw 'language awareness' as an integral part of any bilingual programme, resolving that it should not be isolated from the very experiences which would allow such sensitivity to evolve.

The critical role of attitude and motivation (in implementing language programmes) is also frequently affirmed.[23] To achieve success it is 'vital' that all participants (children, parents, teachers and administrators) should understand the objectives for teaching and learning Welsh. There is, however, an almost naïve belief that 'a clearly stated set of objectives for Welsh' will of itself 'ensure that its place in the curriculum is accepted, understood, valued and willingly implemented'. Whilst conceding that recent research reveals a considerable residual measure of goodwill for the language throughout Wales[24] it is equally apparent, from Government statistics, that this has yet to be translated into general active support. The Report offers little advice on how this might be done, limiting itself instead to noting the general factors governing linguistic success: the school's attitude, supportive teaching, encouragement, enjoyment, but above all the confidence and sense of achievement that comes from being able to use the language. In Welsh, as in French, it seems that 'nothing succeeds like success'.[25]

Problems of implementation

Working within currently available resources, the bilingual goal would, almost certainly, be impossible to attain. To implement the report, therefore, major problems will have to be faced and overcome. The most crucial is a dearth of suitably qualified teachers – the shortfall of Welsh-speaking teachers already being of crisis proportions in some areas of Wales. Add to this the fact that not all Welsh speakers are qualified or able to teach Welsh, and the manpower problem is further considerably compounded. Attempts to ameliorate the situation have already been made. Clwyd, for example, has experimented with concurrent courses (combining Welsh language learning with teaching methodology) for some time. Other authorities have developed intensive 'functional' language learning courses to try to meet their needs. Such developments will require rapid expansion if the Government's curricular targets are ever to be met. A failure to invest, however (in human and financial terms), would render the inclusion of Welsh within the National Curriculum a farce – a sad and inordinate waste of public funds.

It is equally crucial that Welsh should secure an adequate share of time within the curriculum. Successive reports note wide discrepancies in contact time (from as little as a hundred minutes a week to virtually the whole timetable) within Welsh schools. There are numerous reasons why such variations should occur. One is the persistent allegiance of teachers to traditional subject-orientated teaching, and the accompanying view that language learning involves the neglect of other (equally important) educational areas. Language sessions are, therefore, timetabled both in order to ensure that such work is done and so as to maintain a proper balance within the curriculum. The notion that language learning can be an integral part of *any* learning experience is not as widespread as one would like to believe. Even in schools generally regarded as outstanding by the Inspectorate, 'the work in Welsh usually lack[s] relationship to the rest of the curriculum'.[26] In trying to reconcile this reality with the Report's declared aim that a pupil should 'learn enough Welsh to enable him to use it in his everyday life',[27] it soon becomes apparent that the conditions necessary for such ambitious goals to be reached should have received far more attention than they have in the Welsh Working Group Interim Report.

Other basic methodological problems have also been ignored. Teachers in general still have to be convinced that learning a language is somewhat different from learning about the language. In consequence, language-learning is still a relatively passive experience for many learners, the activity being teacher-centred to a considerable extent. The jug and empty vessels syndrome is far from dead. A frequent result is that traditional virtues (associated with the second 'R') are excessively extolled, and characteristics such as speed and accuracy over-stressed at the expense of communication and articulation of thought.

It is, therefore, encouraging to find the Report advocating an approach based on 'enquiry', 'explor[ation]' and 'using' language in 'lively, varied and interesting activities', and to find it stressing that learners learn by so doing – 'the best way to learn how language works is to observe, explore and enquire into its construction as part of the day to day process of learning and using it'.[28] There is also a refreshing inference that perfection and accuracy develop over a period of time (as in first language development) and should not therefore be expected from the very start. Pupils, 'should be encouraged to *try* to convey their thoughts in Welsh, however incomplete and crude the attempt'.[29] The fact that speaking is a social skill involving 'linguistic interaction' is also underlined, as is the importance of creating a healthy attitude 'by means of lively, varied and interesting activities in a happy and relaxed atmosphere'.[30] The general tone of such statements strongly implies that an enquiring, communicative approach is unequivocally endorsed.

Sustained references to such humdrum activities as repetition, imitation, flashcards and the filling of blanks, however, serve to modify the initial impression considerably. The result is a gnawing and lingering feeling that the banal 'linguistic' practices of the past are still alive. Such elements appear often enough in the 'Guidance about targets' to suggest that the methodology implied may not be wholly congruous with the professed aims of the Interim Report.

Such mechanical learning rarely appears in the first language programme, the emphasis being on active language development (under the guidance of a teacher) within meaningful contexts. The exact nature of such experiences, however, is not often revealed and can only be guessed at from sporadic comments within the Report. We glimpse the teacher's role, for example, in the fifth chapter, where he/she is advised to employ 'speech which has been somewhat extended and formalised' and which 'differentiates it slightly from everyday conversation'. But how such statements should be interpreted (on the basis of such slender and elusive evidence) it is very difficult to know. (Is the role, for example, in keeping with Stephen Krashen's 'comprehensible input +1' theory?). A full and elaborate discourse on what are regarded as the main tenets of good language teaching practice would certainly strengthen the final report.

Omissions

Other factors considered crucial to success are periodically and briefly aired. The Report, for example, lays great store on the role of the media in modern linguistic schemes. However, other equally important issues currently facing Welsh teachers are almost completely ignored. One of these is the present hotchpotch of uneven, uncoordinated and disparate teaching material, another the lack of dialogue between producers of radio, magazine, newspaper, and television output and authors of more conventional material. It is interesting, in passing, to note that only at the adult learning level is the multi-media approach considered an important ingredient of success.

The Report makes little reference either to the contribution playgroups can make to ensure linguistic competency, whereas other recent Government reports (for example, Gittins, 1967), deem the institution to have a crucial role to play in promoting bilingual education in Wales:

> The establishment of Welsh voluntary nursery classes in association with *Ysgolion Cymraeg* is of particular significance in bilingual education. These offer the hope of arresting the decline of the Welsh Language and helping to establish bilingualism in Wales.[31]

Gwynedd also gives nursery provision a distinct and central role, seeing it as a means of ensuring that 'through sensitively structured provision and organisation . . . each child receives a firm foundation in Welsh . . . to enable him/her in due course to attain the aim of full bilingualism'.[33] Such affirmations would suggest that the Working Group will have to explore a much more comprehensive language learning approach if its objectives are to be fully realised.

The central role of the adult Welsh learning sector in such plans is also sadly neglected. Yet it would seem to be of paramount importance in order to ensure any measure of bilingual success. Adult support, the cooperation and involvement of those currently, or previously, learning Welsh could prove to be the crucial factor when implementing the National Curriculum, enabling it either to enjoy or be deprived of essential public support.

The Report's main weakness, however, is that it has deferred judgement on so many central issues: how pupils may move from one group to another, the way in which the new targets correspond to the present GCSE, the curriculum suitable for those not taking GCSE, the interim arrangements for pupils whose schools have not hitherto introduced them to Welsh. These are all issues that require immediate and detailed attention. It can only be hoped that the Government's haste to implement the new Education Act will not deny the Working Group the time it needs to deliberate upon such momentous issues. A failure to get the National Curriculum right would almost certainly sound the death knell of the oldest living autochthonous language in the British Isles.

Note
I am grateful to my colleagues Dr C R Baker and Dr B L Davies for reading the first draft of this contribution and making constructive suggestions.

The Basis of Choice

Caroline Filmer-Sankey

As the various contributions to this book demonstrate, many arguments can be put forward in favour of teaching a variety of languages in British secondary schools. The needs of industry and commerce for different languages, the numbers of speakers of various languages in the world, the most frequent holiday destinations for English tourists, and, of course, the advent of the single European Market in 1992, are among the factors which will colour to a certain extent the debate as to which languages should be offered as first foreign languages on the school curriculum. In the preceding chapters, and elsewhere,[1] the merits of a number of the most commonly taught languages in these respects have been examined. In addition to this, studies have been carried out to investigate the feasibility, in terms of organisation, of introducing languages other than French as first foreign languages.[2] As a complement to this kind of information, attention is given in what follows to the question which must be uppermost in the minds of teachers and parents: will secondary school learners progress as well in languages other than French as they do in French itself?

This section is, therefore, centred on the pupil perspective, and looks at a number of factors which may affect the rate and extent of pupils' learning: firstly, the intrinsic difficulty of various languages, in so far as it can be determined, and secondly, the question of the attitudes of pupils towards them. The contribution will conclude with a report on recent research in these areas. The choice of a language ought in part at least to be an educational one. The aim of what follows is not to laud one language above any other, but rather to provide those who are concerned with the issue of diversification with some information, based on educational criteria, which may be of use in deciding which language to offer.

Language difficulty

One question which is central to the debate as to which language should be on offer in schools and which, at the same time, is probably the most intangible, is that of language difficulty. At a time when a language is to be brought into the compulsory curriculum, this is certainly a question which will cross the minds of those who make decisions about language provision. When all but a few pupils up to the age of sixteen are to be taught a foreign language, it would make sense to ensure that the language on offer to them is one in which they are able to progress and achieve and thus that it is not significantly more difficult than any other languages which might be offered.

What, though, do we mean when we say that a language is difficult? Most of the widespread, and albeit subjective views on the relative difficulty of languages are founded on factors intrinsic to the languages themselves. It is not unusual to be told that German grammar is complex or that Spanish vocabulary is easy to learn. There is a tendency to ignore the fact, however, that a language does not become 'difficult' or 'easy' until someone tries to learn it and that its accessibility, therefore, depends as much on the learner's ability, native language, and language learning experience as on any purely linguistic factors. In the school context, for example, the time allocated to languages, the skills of individual teachers and teaching style, and the availability of resources, among other things, will all determine how 'difficult' or 'easy' the language is for the learner. In what follows, therefore, consideration will be given both to difficulties intrinsic to a number of languages and to factors which relate more closely to the language learner's experience. First of all, however, something must be said about the nature of difficulty itself.

Hawkins, whilst conceding that difficulty is an elusive concept, is able to isolate two chief sources of learner error:

(1) the contrasts *between* languages which lead to transfer errors or 'inter-language' interference
(2) the contradictions *within* the foreign language itself which lead to analogical errors or 'intra-language' interference.[3]

'Inter-language' contrasts are examined in some detail by C V James in his study of linguistic distance.[4] He attempts to score five major European languages according to a scale of difficulty ranging from one to five, with regard to phonology, grammar, lexis, orthography, and spelling. A higher score indicates greater distance from English. James's estimates are shown in the table below:

	French	German	Italian	Russian	Spanish
Phonological	4	2	1	3	2
Grammatical	2	3	2	3	2
Lexical	1	2	1	4	1
Spelling	4	2	1	2	1
Orthographic	1	1	1	4	1
Totals	12	10	6	16	7

His overall table of distance shows a sequence (from most to least accessible) of Italian – Spanish – German – French – Russian. This is interesting in that it reflects, apart from Russian, exactly the reverse order of frequency of the teaching of these languages in British schools. However, as James admits, the study is essentially subjective and not research-based. It also fails to take account of the fact, as Eric Hawkins points out, that 'degree of distance does not always coincide with degree of difficulty':[5] an inconsistent or small distance between the mother tongue and the foreign language might cause more learning difficulties than a large, clear and consistent distance. This was a point made as early as 1899, when Henry Sweet warned about the dangers of assuming that the nearer a foreign language is to the mother tongue, the easier it will be: cross-associations between languages will hinder the learner from gaining an accurate knowledge of the foreign language and cognates might prove to be misleading:

> We are naturally inclined to assume that the nearer the foreign language is to our own, the easier it is . . . But this very likeness is often a source of confusion.[6]

Eric Hawkins also points out that it might be easier to cross a given linguistic distance in one direction than in another.[7] To take one random example: an English learner, confronted with the grammatical concept of gender in the foreign language, may find it harder to learn the various article and adjective endings than a German or French person learning the same point in English. Hawkins presents examples from Mandarin Chinese, Danish and English: where the Chinese verb has one form only, the English verb has several, and so a Chinese speaker may face more difficult problems, in this particular case, in learning English, than an English speaker learning Chinese. Similarly, in Danish the present tense possesses one single form whereas English verbs have several different forms and inflections. On the other hand, the English second person pronoun 'you' is used with singular and plural verb forms, whereas Danish speakers have to select between at least three second person pronouns according to the degree of formality of the utterance.[8]

What importance, then, does the concept of 'linguistic distance' have in an assessment of the relative difficulty of various languages? The contrastive hypothesis, reported by Edwin Hopkins, states:

> The base language of the learner influences his acquisition of a second language in as much as elements and rules which are identical are easy to learn and do not cause predisposition to error, while differing elements and rules on the other hand represent learning difficulties and lead to errors.[9]

But Hopkins points out that it does not account for all mistakes in language learning. In the area of phonology it may well be that most errors of pronunciation could be attributed to interference from the phonological system of the learner's language in that sounds which are unfamiliar or slightly dissimilar will prove difficult for the learner. However, the question as to whether the contrastive hypothesis may be extended to morphological, syntactic and semantic errors is debatable. Structural differences between languages, for example, are not necessarily learning difficulties, nor do they inevitably lead to error. Hopkins, Hawkins and Sweet all suggest that it may well be the *lack* of contrast between languages which poses the problems.

The second chief source of error mentioned by Hawkins is 'intra-language' interference or internal contradictions in the foreign language. He feels that the learner's confidence is far more likely to be undermined by this than by 'inter-language' interference. Inconsistencies might be something as simple as 'illogical' gender, for example, *das Messer* (knife), *die Gabel* (fork) and *der Löffel* (spoon) in German, or structural inconsistencies, for which Hawkins[10] refers to the following example:

It's hot (weather)   *il fait chaud*
It's hot (coffee)   *il est chaud*
He's hot (person)   *il a chaud*

The extent to which such contradictions, inconsistencies and illogical constructions create difficulties for the learner will of course depend not only on their complexity and on the stage at which they appear, but also on the ability of the learner: an advanced learner, for example, may be able to cope with inconsistencies which baffle a beginner. Certainly, those languages with internal contradictions in the early stages will present more difficulties for the vast majority of foreign language learners in schools.

What, therefore, are the 'inter-language' and 'intra-language' difficulties, which the languages most commonly taught in British schools (French, German and Spanish) present to the English learner?

In terms of 'inter-language' difficulties in the three languages, C V James's table places Spanish closest to English, with German next and French the most distant. Similarly, when talking about 'intra-language' difficulties or analogical inconsistencies, Hawkins reports:

> Experience of learning these three languages and attempting to teach two of them suggest that French comes first in order of analogical inconsistencies. Spanish certainly has strong claims to be considered easiest in the early stages, with German second.[11]

What aspects of French, then, account for its poor rating in terms of 'inter-language' and 'intra-language' difficulties, as compared with German and Spanish in particular? James's scale shows phonology and spelling to be the areas where French is most distant from English. Language distance and 'inter-language' interference may indeed pose problems in all three languages because the learner has to make sounds to which he is not accustomed, such as nasal sounds in French, vowels modified by *Umlaut* in German and the pronunciation of **v** and **b** in Spanish. 'Intra-language' interference, on the other hand, is clearly most troublesome in French, where the relation between the spoken and written language is weakest. Eric Hawkins shows, in the following examples, how a sound may be spelt in a number of ways:

[lev] spelt: *lève, lèves, lèvent*
[dy] spelt: *du, dû, due, dus, dues, dut, dût*

and

[e]	[E]
é	*è*
et	*ê*
ai	*est*
ez	*ais*
er	*ait*
ed	*ell*
ef	*ett*
	enne
	ess
	mer(ci)
	(jou)et

He also indicates how spelling is no clue to pronunciation, particularly with names of persons and places.[12] The inconsistent use of double consonants (*addition* but *adresse, commission* but *comité, litanie* but *littérature*,[13] is one which does not, for example, occur in Spanish, where a double consonant is never used for a single sound, for example, *acomodar, asociación, atracción.* Conversely, pronunciation is no clue to spelling. Anne Keene quotes the following words with silent endings: *dans, pont, aliments, porte, foulard.*[14] Wilga Rivers demonstrates how written clues to meaning are lost when presented orally and gives examples of person and number of verb: *ils portent*; plurality: *de bons fromages*, and gender: *tout autre, toute autre, quelle bonne amie.*[15]

German and Spanish, on the other hand, exhibit a closer match between sound and written symbol, as is demonstrated in the work of Keene[16] and Bello.[17] The importance of a close match is emphasised by Eric Hawkins: it builds confidence in the language and aids the transition from speaking/hearing skills to reading/writing skills in the foreign language. The written form, moreover, will provide a visual reinforcement to support the growing load on the learner's memory.[18]

While French presents its difficulties, according to James, in the areas of phonology and spelling, German exhibits its complexities in its grammar. Karl Breul, writing at the beginning of this century, lists the common difficulties of German as follows: prepositions and cases, adjectival inflection, modification of root vowels in plurals, comparisons and derivatives, strong and weak declensions, strong and separable verbs, word order and gender.[19] Of these, word order, case and gender perhaps pose most problems because they are not known in the English language.

Where it is normally sufficient for an English learner to transfer his unconscious feel for English sentence structure to French or Spanish, a German clause may be arranged in a number of different ways. In his study of the grammar of English and German, Kufner shows five different patterns of word order:

(1) *Herr Meyer fährt jeden Morgen in die Stadt*

(2) *Jeden Morgen fährt Herr Meyer in die Stadt*
(3) *In die Stadt fährt Herr Meyer jeden Morgen* (all statements)
(4) *Fährt Herr Meyer jeden Morgen in die Stadt?* (question)
(5) *Herr Meyer jeden Morgen in die Stadt fährt* (dependent clause)[20]

Inflection is another area where problems specific to German arise: English learners are already familiar with inflection for number, but not with inflection for case. Bello demonstrates clearly how inflection complicates German for the learner by quoting articles and adjectives as examples. The whole question of inflection, however, is further complicated in German by gender:

> German's manipulation of three genders by four cases is a clear example of the kind of thing that can soon dishearten a beginner.[21]

Gender, moreover, is not generally related to meaning and, although approximate rules can be formulated from spellings, they are not a consistent indicator. This is, of course, no less true of French, as Eric Hawkins demonstrates with a comparison of French and Spanish cognates: the Spanish words clearly indicate gender with their endings (*cigarro* [m], *aduana* [f]) whilst the French words do not (*cigare* [m], *douane* [f]).[22] It is not only German, then, that exhibits complexities at a grammatical level.

Finally, in the area of lexis, James's scores show French and Spanish as equally close to English and German slightly further away. The similar scores for French and Spanish might be explained by the fact that they are both Romance languages. On the other hand, German and English are both Germanic and this makes the direction of James's rating less easy to explain.

In all three languages cognates exist which facilitate language learning. In German these will be encountered at an early stage. Let us take some random examples of nouns and verbs which demonstrate the advantages of cognates:

Banane, Hand, Finger, Arm, Maus, Haus, Garten, Mann, Gras, Buch

trinken, finden, kosten, scheinen, schwimmen, beginnen, enden, lernen, müssen, singen, sitzen.

In French and Spanish, on the other hand, cognates will be encountered at a later stage. Thus vocabulary in social, political and economic registers used in advanced work will be more accessible. The question, therefore, as to which language displays the most useful set of cognates, can only be seen in relation to the needs of the learner.

Care, however, needs to be taken in the use of cognates. While 'disguised' cognates, once recognised, may facilitate learning, for example: *étrange, écarlate, guerre, château, chat* and *Pfeife, weiß, Woche, Tag, baden*,[23] deceptive cognates or 'false friends' may hinder it: *Gift* in German (poison) or *poisson* in French (fish).

Rippmann, indeed, sees a strong objection to frequent use of cognates in language teaching: while cognates may well ease comprehension of the foreign language because they look like an English word, they are liable to create problems of pronunciation, tempting the learner to transfer English rules to the foreign language, an example of 'inter-language' interference: 'the pupils are inclined to approximate them still more, and to let English pronunciation influence that of the foreign word'.[24]

Furthermore, the meaning of a word in one language may not correspond exactly to that of its cognate in another language, as Kufner writes in his analysis of German and English grammar:

> . . . the ranges of lexical items ('words') exist only in a given language and are uniquely integrated in much the same way as the phonetic ranges of a phoneme have no existence outside a given phonology. We cannot expect, therefore, that the various ranges of a German lexical item (its 'Wortfeld') will correspond to those of an English lexical item.[25]

This whole area is discussed in some detail by Bello.[26]

As has been demonstrated, it is possible on a linguistic level to pinpoint difficulties in French, German and Spanish which might pose problems for the English learner, and there is no doubt that this could be done with any other language. As Henry Sweet suggests: 'Learning a language means overcoming difficulties and each language has its own difficulties'.[27] A discussion of contrasts *between* languages will show areas of potential error and a look at the inconsistencies *within* languages will reveal potential sources of confusion. However, as Hopkins points out, contrastive analysis fails to take account of the learner's own process of language acquisition, as it

> can no longer be carried out as a purely linguistic exercise but must be embedded in the learning process and with the learner – in as well as out of school – and his learning processes embedded in it.[28]

This must also be true of the other source of error defined by Hawkins, 'intra-language' interference.

Hopkins alludes above to two factors which also need to be taken into account when considering how difficult a language is: the learner and his or her own process of language acquisition. These, however, are not the only other factors one must consider. The difficulty of a language rests on a wide variety of factors which may be grouped as follows:

(1) the linguistic difficulty;
(2) factors associated with the language learning environment;
(3) factors associated with the learner himself.

Factors associated with the language learning environment, for example, will determine to a great extent how difficult a language proves to be for particular classes or individuals. In the school context, physical factors such as the size of teaching group, the length, timing and frequency of language lessons and the availability of resources will all play a part. In addition to this, the composition of the language class and its group dynamics will affect what and how much is learnt. Finally, the teacher will contribute to the difficulty of the language, both in his/her relationship with the pupils and organisation of the class and in his/her particular teaching methods. A teaching method or style which emphasises difficulties specific to certain languages in the early stages, may make these languages more 'difficult' than one which minimises them. German, for example, traditionally thought to be grammatically complex, may be 'easier' when taught communicatively:

> Beginners do not need to understand the grammatical structures in order to know what to say or to understand what is said to them.[29]

Similarly, French may be made more difficult by an overemphasis on the written skill because the written language, as has been indicated above briefly, is fraught with apparent inconsistencies. This will apply as well to the course book used, in that differing emphases may highlight or play down potential sources of error.

The way in which the language is presented to the learner, then, will be as important a factor in determining how difficult the language appears as the intrinsic difficulty of the language itself. This was shown by the findings from a small-scale survey of older pupils' attitudes carried out in the Oxford area, where it was found that pupils were most influenced by the nature of their learning experience:

> Nor was it usually according to the nature of the language that pupils measured accessibility. Some pupils, for example, found one language easier simply because they preferred it and therefore worked harder at it. Others were more influenced by teaching methods and the length of the course.[30]

More recently, this has been corroborated by the findings from a survey of the attitudes of first-year pupils learning French, German and Spanish carried out in 1988 by the Oxford Project on Diversification of First Foreign Language Teaching (OXPROD), which will be discussed in more detail below. When asked to say why they found the language they were learning easy or difficult, comments about the teacher and lesson content were more common than comments on specific language difficulties.

The third group of factors to be considered are those associated with the learner himself. The learner's native language, for example, will determine the extent and nature of 'inter-language' interference which the learner has to surmount. The learner's previous experience of language learning will affect the way he appoaches a new language as well as his attitudes towards the language learning process. His general ability and language learning aptitude will also be important. Ann Miller points out, for example, that different kinds of ability might be required for learning different languages: French taxes the memory of the English speaker in the early stages of vocabulary learning whilst German makes a demand upon his feeling for the functions of words in sentences.[31] There is also the highly complex question of the learner's natural process of language acquisition which will vary in effectiveness according to the language taught and the method used. Finally, there is the whole question of the learner's own perceptions of difficulty and his attitudes towards the language and language learning generally, which will be the subject of later sections.

Pupil attainment

Another perspective on the question of language difficulty is that of pupil attainment. The choice of a language would be made much easier if one could find valid answers to such questions as:

Do girls attain better in German than in French?
Will our low ability pupils progress better if we offer them Spanish?
Will our high ability boys achieve better results in German at GCSE than they would in French?

Unfortunately, this is not as simple as it might appear. A brief glance at public examination statistics for the last decade might afford insights into the numbers of pupils entered for each language at 16+ level and the distributions of scores across the various languages taught in secondary schools. However, they will merely show how well pupils have achieved on certain tests and will not be hard evidence that learners will achieve better results in any one language than another. An enormous number of factors, including learning conditions, teaching styles and pupil aptitudes, will all have a bearing on what is attained in such tests. Indeed, differing methods of assessment, from pupil profiling on the one hand to testing on the other, with the associated problems of subjectivity in the former and of test comparability in the latter, simply will not allow fair comparisons to be made between the languages.

With these limitations in mind, it might be more useful for those who require some sort of information on pupil attainment in different languages to look within languages at specific areas where pupils have been shown to achieve.

Extensive work of this kind on attainment, mainly in French, has been carried out since 1983 by the Assessment of Performance Unit (APU) in their large-scale surveys of pupil performance (1985, 1986 and 1987).[32]

The earliest survey examined levels of attainment across the whole ability range in French, German and Spanish when taught as first foreign languages. The pupils included were a sample of those who reached the age of thirteen in the school year in which each survey took place.

Attainment was tested discretely in the four language learning skills of listening, speaking, reading and writing, and in eighteen topic areas such as 'food and drink' and 'shopping'. For a number of reasons, not least the virtual impossibility of designing tests of comparable difficulty in the three languages, the APU were unable to make absolute comparisons between French, German and Spanish.

They were able to say, however, that the main characteristics of pupils' performance did not differ substantially from one language to another: in each language pupils were successful in the same topics and tasks. It was remarked, however, that a pattern in German of higher scores in listening than in reading contrasted with results in French and Spanish:

the strong suggestion that English-speaking pupils find the phonological system in German more accessible, because there are more recognisable and consistent associations with the written language, is supported by the finding that German listening was one of only two areas in which the performance of pupils whose first foreign language was not English was significantly lower than that of English speaking pupils.[33]

Researchers, teachers and pupils have all remarked on this characteristic of German.[34]

In the future, of course, it may well be more meaningful to examine carefully the attainment scores (GCSE results, for example) of pupils in various languages in schools which have truly diversified and where languages other than French are well established. For the moment, however, information on attainment can only be taken as a superficial way of gaining some measure of the accessibility of various languages. By itself, it provides little useful information on which to base the choice.

An altogether more fruitful avenue is the question of pupil attitude. This has been found by researchers to be an important factor affecting pupil attainment and must therefore have implications for the choice of language. The next section will examine this in some detail.

Attitude

While it is enormously difficult to assess pupil achievement accurately and to make comparisons across languages, it is only too clear to any language teacher, particularly when languages are in the core curriculum, whether pupils are well or badly motivated in their language lessons. Perhaps one of the most crucial areas to be considered when making decisions about which language to offer in school, therefore, is that of pupil attitudes.

The question of motivation is one which can be viewed from several different perspectives. For example, do pupils have different attitudes towards various languages even before they start learning them, which might subsequently affect the way they learn, or are they better (or less well) motivated when taught languages other than French as first foreign languages, or do some pupils (e.g. boys or high ability pupils) respond better to some languages than others? These are all questions which merit some consideration before decisions are made as to which language is most suitable as a first foreign language.

Previous work on attitudes towards language learning has isolated three main areas of attitude:

(1) attitudes which precede the learner's approach to foreign language learning;
(2) attitudes towards the learning situation itself;
(3) attitudes resulting from the learning experience.

The first two of these areas were investigated by Gardner and Lambert,[35] and by the National Foundation for Educational Research (NFER), under the direction of Burstall.[36]

Gardner and Lambert were concerned with the role of attitudes in a twelve-year series of studies of language learning in North America and developed the theory that motivation to learn a language is determined by the learner's attitudes towards the people who speak that language, by his attitudes towards foreign people in general and by his orientation to the language learning task itself. They distinguished between two kinds of motivation, 'integrative' and 'instrumental', arguing that motivation is 'integrative' if the student wants to learn more about the language and culture of another community because of a sincere and personal interest in it and 'instrumental' if the purposes of his language study reflect a utilitarian value.

The importance of these two aspects of motivation was also examined in an NFER longitudinal survey of pupil attitudes towards language learning in primary and secondary schools from 1964 to 1974.[37] Two of the stated aims of the survey were to investigate the long-term development of pupils' attitudes towards foreign language learning and to discover whether pupils' levels of achievement in French were significantly related to their attitudes towards language learning, taking into account pupil variables such as sex, age, socio-economic status, perceptions of language learning and contact with France. Evidence was gathered to suggest that a positive association did exist between pupils' levels of achievement and their attitudes towards French. In addition to this, it was found that successful experience of language learning also promoted future success:

> Attitudes towards learning French are, in any case, less reliable predictors of later achievement in French than early achievement is: *in the language-learning context, nothing succeeds like success.*[38]

It has also been suggested[39] that attitudes and motivation, as examined in the Gardner and Lambert and NFER studies, should be considered against more generalised attitudes or personality factors. In addition to the factors of 'integrative' and 'instrumental' motivation, Krashen, who makes the distinction between subconscious language *acquisition* and conscious language *learning*, identifies self-confidence and empathy as factors which affect the rate of language acquisition. The self-confident person will be more able to encourage intake and the empathic person may be able to identify more easily with speakers of the target language. He argues that positive attitudes are important for both language *acquisition* and language *learning* and that they produce two effects:

> they encourage useful input for language acquisition and they allow the language acquirer to be 'open' to this input so that it can be utilised for acquisition.[40]

Another factor which he identifies is that of attitudes to the classroom and teacher: not only do positive attitudes of this kind encourage acquisition but also he would expect students with such attitudes to apply themselves better in class and therefore consciously to learn more.

As has been shown, Gardner and Lambert and Burstall were concerned firstly with conditions which precede the learner's approach to foreign language learning. These include the learner's motives for learning the language ('integrative' and 'instrumental'), attitudes towards the community and people who speak the language, and more generalised attitudes such as interest in foreign languages and personality. Secondly, they were interested in attitudes towards the learning situation itself. These include attitudes towards the teacher and the language course, and parents' attitudes.

Stern adds a third area: 'the affective conditions that ultimately *result* from the learning experience and the learning outcome,[41] which must be considered when viewing attitude as a whole. In other words, are pupils more positive about language learning if their experience has been of one language rather than another?

There are, thus, clearly defined areas which must be considered when attempting to compare pupil attitudes towards *different* languages. In determining how well motivated the pupils are, their inbuilt attitudes towards the country and people of the language concerned and their perceptions of the usefulness of learning specific languages must be examined alongside their enjoyment of the language and perceptions of its difficulty and, finally, the attitudes which result from the whole learning experience.

Work which has examined the attitudinal area across a number of languages, taking into account the factors discussed above, has been carried out in recent years by the APU and OXPROD.

The work of the APU, while mainly focussed on pupil attainment, is of considerable interest in the study of pupil attitudes across the languages. Within the framework of a large-scale survey of foreign language performance carried out in 1983 they investigated and compared 13 year old pupils' attitudes to learning French, German, and Spanish by means of an attitude questionnaire.[42] Particular areas examined were pupils' enjoyment of the foreign language, their perceptions of its difficulty and usefulness, and their attitudes towards the foreign community.

Several factors inhibited absolute comparisons between pupils' attitudes towards the three languages:

(1) the sample of pupils was not entirely representative as the numbers of pupils learning German and Spanish were much smaller and concentrated in fewer schools;

(2) a far greater proportion of pupils learning French than of those learning German or Spanish had more than three years' experience of the language;

(3) owing to the very large scale of the work it was not feasible to take into account other important variables such as the ability of the pupils, the course books used and teaching styles.

However, some extremely valuable evidence, particularly in favour of Spanish and German, was gathered. For each language the following general conclusion was drawn:

> more pupils thought that the foreign language was useful, enjoyable and not difficult than the contrary;

more pupils wanted contact with the foreign community than not;

higher proportions of girls than boys had positive views on all these aspects;

higher proportions of those who had visited the foreign country than those who had not, had positive attitudes.[43]

Furthermore, interesting differences were shown between the three languages:

the highest proportion of both girls and boys finding the foreign language useful, was among pupils learning Spanish;

the highest proportion of both girls and boys finding the foreign language easy and enjoyable, was among pupils learning German;

the highest proportion of girls wanting contact with the foreign community, was in German. The highest proportions of boys were in French and German.[44]

The evidence of this work suggests, then, that pupils were *at least* as positively motivated when taught a language other than French as first foreign language, if not more so. This is a trend examined further by OXPROD, which, by dint of its much smaller scale, is able to look more closely at the variables affecting attitude which have been described above. In the next section that work, which looks closely at the question of attitude, is examined in some detail.

The Oxford Project on Diversification of First Foreign Language Teaching

The four-year Oxford Project on Diversification of First Foreign Language Teaching, which started its work in January 1987, and which is funded primarily by the Leverhulme Trust, aims to test the hypothesis that there is nothing in the nature of German or Spanish as subjects in the school curriculum that makes these languages unsuitable as first foreign languages for the whole ability range. The research is focussed on three main questions:

What *attitudes* do children have to French, German and Spanish at various stages of their learning?

What *difficulties* do children experience in French, German and Spanish at which stages of their learning?

What *organisational problems* are evident in the project schools that result from teaching a language other than French as first foreign language?

In the area of attitude, the project's aim is to examine which aspects of French, German and Spanish pupils find most useful, interesting and enjoyable, what they think about the activities in which they are involved in their lessons and what they think about the people and country of the language they are learning. It also aims to investigate changes in pupils' attitudes over the first three years of secondary school and to examine how attitudinal differences are related to the ability and sex of the pupils. The kinds of questions OXPROD hopes to explore are, to take two random examples, do high ability boys respond better to Spanish than to German, or do girls in general enjoy Spanish more than French? Pupils' perceptions of the difficulty of the various languages are, of course, an integral part of their attitudes.

The main investigation into attitudes started in September 1987 with first-year pupils in six project schools offering French and at least one other foreign language in parallel. In 1987–88 three of the project schools offered French and German, one offered French and Spanish, one French, German and Spanish and the sixth, French, German and Italian. At the time of writing (1989) the pupils involved in the project have completed their second year and some have started a second foreign language.

As the project is still in progress, much of the data-gathering and its analysis has not yet been carried out. This includes work on the development of pupil attitudes over the three years. Some interesting conclusions can be drawn, however, on first-year pupils' attitudes towards the various languages.

In common with the other research studies already described, it was decided in OXPROD to investigate pupil attitudes by means of a questionnaire. The questionnaire which was developed for use in the first year drew on two questionnaires already in existence: the questionnaire designed for the Schools Council Project on Graded Objectives in 1981[45] and the questionnaire developed at the National Foundation for Educational Research for the APU for use in their surveys of foreign language performance and attitude.[46]

It covered the following areas:

(1) pupils' general attitudes to and enjoyment of French, German and Spanish;
(2) their views on the usefulness of the language they were learning;
(3) their perceptions of the difficulty of the language they were learning;
(4) their attitudes to the country and people of the language they were learning;
(5) their enjoyment of language learning activities;
(6) factual information about their contact with the foreign country.

Areas (1) to (4) were investigated together in one section of the questionnaire, which incorporated Likert-type scales. Groups of statements were presented which indicated positive or negative attitudes towards the four factors. The findings discussed below are based on the analysis of this section. The remaining sections, including an open-ended section where pupils wrote a comment in response to several statements about the language, provided useful contextual information.

The questionnaire was administered to approximately 1,000 first-year pupils in the project schools in March 1988 (52% learning French, 34% German, 12% Spanish, 2% Italian) and a statistical analysis was carried out to compare pupils' attitudes to each of the four languages with which OXPROD is concerned, the attitudes of boys and girls, and the attitudes of those who had been to the country and those who had not.

The main findings from the pupil attitude questionnaire will be presented here, without full details of the statistical analysis which are published elsewhere.[47]

The main analyses were based on four scales which reflected pupils' views on:

(1)   the enjoyment derived from learning a foreign language;
(2)   the perceived difficulty;
(3)   the usefulness of learning a foreign language;
(4)   the wish for contact with the people of the country of the language being learnt.

As might be expected with pupils at a relatively early stage in their language learning, higher proportions of pupils held positive rather than negative views in all the areas examined. More pupils found the language they were learning enjoyable, easy and useful than did not, and more pupils wished for contact with the foreign community than not.

When attitudes towards the various languages were compared, some very interesting findings were revealed. In terms of the pupils' enjoyment, their perceptions of the difficulty and usefulness of the language and their attitudes towards the foreign community, the three languages could be ranked in the order German – Spanish – French, pupils on the whole being shown to be most positive about German and least positive about French. In fact, in all but one area (that relating to the usefulness of the languages) these differences were statistically significant.

A higher proportion of the pupils learning German than of those learning French enjoyed it rather than not and similarly, more of the pupils learning German than of those learning French perceived it to be easy rather than not. This corroborated the APU's findings that 'the highest proportions of both girls and boys finding the foreign language easy and enjoyable, was among pupils learning German'.[48] It was particularly interesting to note that this bias was attributable solely to the attitudes of the boys: whereas girls learning French and German were equally positive, boys learning German were significantly more positive than boys learning French.

In the same way, whilst all pupils were interested in going to the country or meeting the people who speak the language they were learning, more pupils learning German wished for contact with the foreign community than pupils learning French. In this case, it was the girls who tipped the balance in favour of German, higher proportions wishing for contact with Germany than with France. The APU had also found girls to be most positive about German in this respect.[49]

In all areas except for pupils' views on contact with the foreign community (where girls were more positive than boys), there were no statistically significant differences between the attitudes of girls and boys, though girls' attitudes were marginally better when viewed as a whole. On the other hand, when the views of specific *groups* of pupils were examined, it was found that boys learning German were the most positive of all. It would, of course, be dangerous to say that these findings are generalisable to all first-year pupils, as the sample of schools is not representative, and other variables, in particular the teachers involved, will have considerable influence. The differences in attitude do, nonetheless, invite further examination.

In an open-ended section of the questionnaire pupils were given the opportunity to express reasons for their responses. To some extent, their comments were predictable and similar across the languages. Nearly half the pupils overall, for example, mentioned the teacher or the way they were taught as the main reason why they enjoyed or did not enjoy the language, and this was also an important factor in determining how easy or difficult they found the language. The following comments are typical of the views expressed (G = girl, B = boy):

I really like French. . . . My teacher is really great. She helps me and I understand her. (G)

I think whether you enjoy French lessons or dislike them depends on what teacher you have. You're learning a new language and you're uncertain and need someone to approach the lesson in a fun way and help you enjoy it. (G)

It depends whether you have a good teacher or not. If the teacher is boring, German is boring. If the teacher is good, German is good. It just so happens our teacher is boring. (G)

I like Spanish because we get to do a lot of different things, writing about ourselves is good fun but just generally I like learning something different. (B)

I think German is an interesting subject because of the teacher. It all depends on what the teacher does and how he or she explains the subject. (B)

I find French quite easy because it's made fun. *Bibliobus*[50] and *Tricolore*[51] and games and puzzles make it easy. (B)

The perceived difficulty of the language was an important factor in determining how much it was enjoyed. Pupils expressed ideas about the relative difficulty of various languages without necessarily having experience of more than one. Many of their comments were based on hearsay:

German is the easiest foreign language. (B)

French is more simple and doesn't have all those ichs in them because you end up spitting. (Girl learning French only)

German is an easy language compared with French and Spanish. (B)

French sounds harder and there is more to learn in it. (B)

German is easier than French – that is what everyone has told me. (B)

My brother says German is easier than French. (B)

People say that other languages are harder than Spanish. (G)

My teacher says French is easy and the others aren't. (B)

A large proportion of pupils were able to say what exactly they found difficult. In some cases linguistic difficulties were mentioned (which will be discussed later) and in others the fact that they had not done a language before affected their perceptions: many pupils pointed out that languages were more difficult than other subjects because they had not studied them at primary school. Similarly, a fair proportion of pupils pointed out that languages were difficult because they were *different* from other school subjects, other subjects being taught in English. Many pupils expressed comments similar to the ones put by these pupils:

You speak English in other lessons. (B)

It's a different language. In other lessons it is English and we can understand all right but in French we have to learn it like we had to learn English when we were younger. (G)

Predictably, comments about the usefulness of the languages centred around job prospects and holidays. Those pupils who had already decided on a career, held firm views about the necessity of having foreign languages, as the following random and bizarre comments illustrate:

I want to be a football player and if I do I might get bought from Spain, so it would be helpful to know the language. (B)

When I grow up I want to become a policeman. What use is German to a policeman? (B)

I want to work with horses and I don't think they speak Spanish. (G)

On a more general note, pupils were well aware that a language (but not any particular one) would be an asset when making a job application and would qualify them for better paid jobs:

Quite a few jobs are better if you know another language. (G)

In the same way that pupils held ideas about the relative *difficulty* of the various languages, they also held strong views (many incorrect) on the relative *importance* of the various languages, to take a few examples:

More people speak German than French or Spanish. (G)

French is a more universal language than German or Spanish. (B)

German is the second most spoken language. (G)

As far as holidays and contact with the foreign country were concerned, pupils were generally very positive about the languages, especially where a link already existed with the country (for example, a time-share flat or a relative) or where there was the prospect of a visit there in the near future. Very few pupils expressed prejudicial views about the countries or the people.

The following comments are typical of the few negative views which were expressed:

Spanish is a waste of time because they speak good English over there. (B)

I'm glad I haven't been to France. I hate the smell there. I hate French a lot. (B)

I want to be a cook, not a French-speaking person out of work. French does not get jobs. (B)

While the attitudinal trends discussed above are of interest in themselves, no particular bias towards any one language was revealed in them which might corroborate the statistical analysis.

Let us now turn to three areas where it *was* possible to detect clear differences in attitude.

Firstly, pupils learning languages other than French were pleased to be doing something new and different from the language normally taught:

I'm glad I'm learning Italian because I feel proud as it is not usually learnt in most schools. (G)

Spanish is a new language taught in schools and we got the chance to study it for the first time. (B)

[Spanish] is a different language to ours and not many other schools do it in the first year. (B)

[German] is a different thing to do. At most schools first-years have to do French. (G)

I am not glad I am learning French. I would rather learn something different like Spanish or German. (B)

I'm glad I am learning German rather than French because everyone knows bits of French and it is easy. (G)

Secondly and in contrast, pupils learning French mentioned the fact that their parents or siblings had learnt it and were pleased because they could help them with homework:

I am glad I'm doing French because if I get stuck my Mum or brother can help me. (G)

I like French and my sister does French so we can help each other. (G)

I'd rather learn French for my Mum can speak it and I have a French penpal. (G)

And where parental preference was mentioned it was almost always for French:

My Mum and Dad want me to learn French and some people in my family speak French. (B)

My parents would rather make me learn French. (G)

Encouraging, however, was the fact that this was not the case in those project schools which had a long history of diversification, where siblings had learnt German or where the family already had contact with Germany and Spain. In the case of German, this was frequently through the RAF and in the case of Spanish, because of holidays abroad.

Some pupils learning languages *other* than French were pleased that they were learning a completely different language from that known to their families:

I am the only one in the family learning German. (G)

It's exciting to learn new words and in a way I feel proud because my brother and my sister have learnt French and I'm learning Italian. (G)

All my uncles and aunties and cousins learnt to speak French so I thought I would be different. (B)

The third and most significant area where differences between the various languages were revealed was in pupils' perceptions of the difficulty of the language they were learning. Pupils' comments, on the whole, support the views of theorists and teachers on particular difficulties in each language, which have been discussed above in the section on language difficulty.

The close relationship between the written and spoken language is one which German learners in particular mentioned frequently. The following comments are but a small sample of those on this aspect:

German words are easier to say because you sound almost every letter. (B)

In German when we have a spelling test the words are spelt like you hear them. (B)

I don't think German is hard at all, you sound out the letters in the words and often the words are similar to English words. (G)

I find German easy and the words are easy to pronounce. (B)

Spanish learners thought similarly:

Spanish is probably the easiest language to learn as most of the words are spoken as they look. (G)

These contrast sharply with the following comments about French:

French words don't look easy and are not. (G)

French is harder to pronounce. (G)

French sounds different to what it looks on paper. (B)

I don't like French because of the way they write and the accent. (B)

I think it's hard to say and when you hear it on tape it sounds different in writing. (B)

I think some things are easy like numbers and some hard like verbs and all the different meanings and spellings for one word. (B)

Several pupils referred to difficulties with writing in French, particularly with the accents:

Learning German is easier than French because you don't have to put so many dittos above the letters. (G)

From what I've seen and what other people tell me, French is harder with all the signs above their words. (G)

I find French more difficult than other subjects because of all the verbs and the little squiggles above and below words. (B)

All the verbs and dots and dashes puzzle me. I put them in the wrong order. (B)

Another aspect of German (and, to some extent, Spanish) which received much comment is the incidence of cognates. The following comments are just a few of those on this subject:

In German a lot of words are spelt the same (apart from a few letters in each one) and some words sound the same. (B)

I think that German is nearly the same as English because the Anglo-Saxons came from Germany. (B)

German is a bit similar to English. (G)

I think that German is very easy to understand and I have found that many of their words are very much like ours. (G)

I think I would prefer French because you learn more new words. German is very much like English. (G)

German is quite an easy lesson because quite a lot of German words sound the same or look the same. (G)

Some words are similar to English words. (G)

German sounds vaguely like the English language and it has a nice tang to it. (B)

Spanish is quite easy because most of the words are not unlike our own. (B)

Spanish is easy depending on what I'm doing because the words are not as hard as other foreign words. (B)

None of the pupils learning French mentioned this as an aspect where French was easy.

On a grammatical level pupils learning French, German and Spanish all mentioned areas of particular difficulty. Most of the comments related to the question of gender:

> I don't like the idea of male and female in everything, even rulers. It's silly and confusing. (G) [French learner]

> The *le, la, un,* and *une* are confusing, so are other male and female things. (G)

> Some parts of Spanish are confusing like masculine and feminine. (G)

> There are too many verbs and masculine and feminine words to learn. It is a bit much to make a beginner learn that. (G)

> I think French is easier than German because it sounds nicer and is probably easier to pick up and because it has two genders. (G)

> I would rather learn German because you don't have two words for everything if it's a man or lady. (G)

> I find German difficult because of the verb endings and the three words for 'the'. (G)

> I don't find German hard but some things are a bit hard like *der, die* and *das* words. (G)

> I find the *der, die* and *das, zum* or *zur* words difficult to learn. (G)

The following comments show pupils' frustration with gender when further complicated by case in German:

> I'm not sure about my verbs. It's like learning your alphabet a ber ker dur and then learning it ay bee cee dee!!! There are so many *zum's, zur's, die's, das's* and then *den* comes from *der*. WHY CAN'T GERMAN PEOPLE HAVE ONE WORD LIKE 'THE' instead of about 20 words? (G)

> I don't really like the way she sets us on *ein, eine, einen,* then *der, die, das* then *zums* and *zurs* and now *ein, eine, einen* again. It's confusing! Germans are weird. Or it might just be our teacher! (G)

While one boy pointed out that 'German is easy because there are rules for the words and Germans stick to them and there are no exceptions', the complexities of gender and case were perceived particularly by learners of German to be areas of potential difficulty.

OXPROD's research does, therefore, shed interesting light on what pupils think about French, German and Spanish. In the work undertaken to date it has been shown that first-year pupils are more positive about German than French in terms of their enjoyment, their perceptions of its difficulty and their desire to have contact with Germany and German-speaking people. Some of the areas they perceive to be difficult in each language correspond exactly with areas already acknowledged by experts to be problematic for the English learner. It must be stressed, however, that the work carried out so far is with first-year pupils only. As the pupils grow older and their attitudes change, so will their perceptions of what is difficult in each language. While it is known, for example, that the high incidence of cognates in German facilitates learning in the early stages, complexities of grammar later on may well disillusion the second- or third-year learner.

Finally it is important to reaffirm the fact that pupils were more influenced in their attitudes by their teacher and his or her methods than by the languages themselves. Thus, while the evidence so far provided by OXPROD in favour of various languages is certainly persuasive, it should not be seen as conclusive.

Conclusion

The decision as to which language is offered in school must be based on a number of factors. As it cannot be predicted which of the various languages might be needed by any one pupil in later life, or indeed whether he or she will know them well enough to be able to use them, it would make sense to choose as first foreign languages those with which pupils are most able to cope, which ensure a positive experience of language learning, and which provide them with language learning tools that they can use thereafter.

It has been argued above that languages have different areas of difficulty, so that it is not possible to make absolute comparisons of their accessibility. Similarly, any attempt to compare pupil attainment across the languages is equally problematic.

On the other hand, there is no doubt that pupils do respond differently to various languages and that such considerations must take their place alongside any practical considerations when diversification is being planned. The current research of OXPROD indicates that it is through the assessment of pupil attitudes that these differential responses may best be defined.

INSET and Diversification

Michael Calvert

The introduction of the National Curriculum represents the most significant change in teaching since the advent of the comprehensive system in the 1960s. For modern language teachers the change from the two-tier system meant that almost *all* pupils were to be taught a modern language and not simply the most able minority in the grammar schools. With the new changes, a language is to be offered to all pupils from 11 to 16 rather than its being an optional subject in most schools. In the 1960s, as now, new methodological approaches were being introduced: audio-lingual and audio-visual approaches were replacing the grammar-translation methods; new equipment – language laboratories, tape recorders, slide projectors – was required. At the present time new syllabuses and examinations at all levels, communicative approaches to language learning involving pupil-centred, task-based activities, new equipment in the form of satellite TV and computers/wordprocessors, all present similar challenges.

With hindsight, it is obvious that the typical language teacher of the 1960s was woefully ill-prepared for the changing demands of the new situation. Such a teacher, trained and experienced in using the traditional methods with a selective intake, was likely to experience considerable difficulty in adjusting and, to be frank, some never did. Modern language departments were often ill-prepared and ill-equipped for the organisational and practical demands that the new courses made on them. The HMI report *Modern Languages in Comprehensive Schools* (1977)[1] paints a depressing picture of what had been happening, referring to poor performance by pupils, poor methodology and inadequate schemes of work, and stating that the increase in demand for French teachers resulted in 'an inevitable dilution of quality'. In short, the teachers were unable to be as successful as they might have been. This situation could have been avoided if appropriate in-service training (INSET) had been given.

Fortunately modern language teaching has made great strides forward since then, possibly in part as a result of the 1977 HMI report. Many schools have built up strong departments with a clear policy on language teaching and for which diversification and offering a language to all from 11 to 16 is already a reality or a logical next step in their plans. Not all schools are in this position, and in order that such radical changes can be introduced across the country smoothly, and with maximum benefit to teachers and students alike, it is vital that modern languages has a full and comprehensive system of INSET.

INSET required to help teachers prepare for and introduce the recommendations of the national curriculum can be divided into three categories: linguistic, organisational and methodological.

Language INSET

The introduction of the National Curriculum will dramatically increase the need for language INSET. It is well known that there is a serious shortfall in the number of modern language teachers. The DES currently (1989) estimate the shortfall as 2,500, although some reports estimate that between three and six thousand additional teachers are required to service the National Curriculum. With diversification it is clear that there will be a great demand for teachers offering languages other than French. Many of the teachers required clearly need to be additional to the existing stock, i.e. new entrants to the profession or teachers who have re-trained in modern languages. In reality, however, most efforts are likely to be directed at fully utilising the existing pool of language teachers. As the DES Statement of Policy (1988)[2] revealed, in many schools there are teachers who are not using the languages for which they have been trained or are only using the languages to a very limited extent. Clearly, as Felicity Rees points out,[3] not all of these teachers would be able, nor would necessarily want, to teach the language or to teach it to a greater degree given the opportunity. Nevertheless, her survey reveals that, 'In one third of cases, respondents said they would be prepared to teach [the 'lapsed' language] given improved proficiency or retraining'.[4]

In order to harness the existing potential, there are two possible different types of INSET. The first involves reviving the 'dormant' potential of the 'lapsed linguist'. The 'lapsed linguist' has usually reached a certain level of competence but, by dint of not teaching or using the language, no longer has sufficient mastery to teach it effectively to the level required or the necessary recent knowledge of the country. The second type of training involves offering *ab initio* courses to language teachers in one of the designated languages.

Retraining 'lapsed linguists' is likely to be the priority for many authorities in order for them to meet their short and medium term needs in terms of diversification. The amount of INSET required by each teacher will vary enormously depending on the level of study attained originally, the way in which the language was taught, and the amount of recent practice, if any, either in the classroom or in the country.

Training *ab initio* is likely to respond to the longer term effects of diversification. In the short term a school requires at least two teachers of a language (ideally three) in order to diversify. Over a five-year period, more staffing clearly has to be devoted to the new first foreign language (FL1) as the language moves up the school. This may only involve a small extra commitment at first which does not, in itself, warrant recruiting another member of staff. It may simply require a very flexible staffing arrangement to meet the needs of the timetable. It may well be necessary to cover the extra lessons by existing staff through a teacher learning a new language to a satisfactory level. The benefits of *ab initio* training are not as easily identifiable or quantifiable as those of further training. Changing circumstances within a school/LEA such as falling rolls, amalgamation, opting out, etc., and the usual problems of staff movement, make forecasting long-term staffing needs difficult and do not guarantee that the teacher will still be there to provide the teaching in the new language for which he/she is being trained. Nevertheless, as well as meeting the needs of schools with shortages, *ab initio* courses do provide an opportunity for language teachers to enhance their career prospects by learning a new language. This is particularly important for the monolinguist French teacher, for example, or for the teacher of a minority language not covered by the National Curriculum, who might well find promotion more difficult than a similarly qualified teacher of two main languages.

Having established the need for further training and *ab initio* courses, we need to look at the range of INSET currently available and highlight features of the training which are most important. It will be useful to focus on one authority which is committed to INSET and which offers an impressive programme of courses to its teachers. Lancashire is not alone in offering well-integrated provision but will serve as a focal point for the study.

Lancashire is a large county with approximately 110 secondary schools. It is a county with a well-structured, comprehensive approach to INSET which serves the teachers in the authority and, sometimes, also benefits the teachers working in the metropolitan boroughs such as Bolton, Bury and Rochdale. Lancashire is one of ten LEAs to receive education support grant (ESG) funding and, as such, will receive an extra £27,500 to spend on INSET in the second year of the project (1989–90).[5] However, it must be pointed out that the INSET described below pre-dates for the most part the extra funding made available by the grant and the extra money will mostly be used to extend the existing provision to more teachers, although some innovation is planned.

Within the county there is provision for language training ranging from *ab initio* to degree level courses. There are courses held in the evening, at weekends, five-day and eight-day residential courses, paired intensive days,[6] distance learning packs and residential courses abroad. Naturally these courses are not mutually exclusive. Furthermore, the teachers are able to negotiate which courses would be the most suitable and what level they expect to reach. Local INSET is also used to supplement the provision.[7]

Lancashire uses two centres for a considerable amount of its INSET work: Lancashire Polytechnic and Lancashire College. The former offers degree level courses (Lancashire Polytechnic Diploma) and Institute of Linguists (IoL) courses. Lancashire College has developed considerable expertise in developing training materials for local industries such as ICI and British Aerospace and also prepares teachers for IoL examinations, ICC examinations, BTEC Certificate in Continuing Education (for those attending a two-week residential course), prepares packs for distance learning, and organises residential courses abroad and in its own residential centre. For the purposes of this study we will concentrate on the work of Lancashire College, which provides the majority of the courses used by teachers in the authority.

Lancashire College offers courses at seven levels from *ab initio* to IoL final examinations. The teachers at the College are taught in groups of ten by native speakers, wherever possible. In order to produce viable groups, teachers are sometimes taught with other language learners. Before attending a course some teachers (and other learners, of course) may take advantage of one of the distance learning packs. This involves their working on ten units, selected from a bank of materials which correspond to their needs and to the level of the course. The teachers then work on the material and send their oral work on tape to their personal tutor. The teachers are entitled to fifteen minutes contact with their tutor after each unit. This time can be pooled, i.e. two teachers can get together and double their contact time and some teachers prefer to meet after every two units for half an hour. Contact can be made by telephone instead if preferred. Working on the units in this way enables the teachers who intend to follow up their study with a residential course to know what the level required is and, if necessary, spend extra time preparing in order to be able to progress comfortably to the next level. If the level proves to be too easy or difficult the material and the course level can be changed. The arrangements are flexible; a beginner might prefer to do a distance learning course before a residential course at the next level or may prefer to do two residential courses and not take advantage of the distance learning pack.

All the courses involve the use of the foreign language throughout – even at meal times. The approach is communicative and the pace is accelerated. Teachers on *ab initio* courses can reach the level of the Lancashire Graded Test Level 3 in three to five days, and an eight-day course will take a beginner to a level equivalent to GCSE Higher Level in all the skill areas.

In addition to the residential courses held at the College there are courses organised abroad. For example, the College is planning a two-week residential course for teachers of German. The teachers spend the first week at the College and then travel to Germany for the second week. They exchange places with a group of German teachers learning English. Given the reciprocal nature of the arrangements, both for accommodation and tuition, costs are considerably reduced.

Having described in outline some of the courses, let us now consider a number of features in more detail.

The most important aspect is flexibility. It enables teachers with different social, domestic and professional commitments to choose the sort of INSET which most corresponds to their needs. It allows teachers to reach a number of different levels from a variety of starting points. The distance learning packs have the added advantage of being able to level out differences of ability and experience within the group by motivating individuals to reach a particular level of competence and knowledge before attending a course.

On the subject of motivation there are a number of important points to be made:

(1) Teachers benefit from working in homogeneous groups. Very often local INSET has to cater for a wide range of ability in one group to ensure viability, whereas the College manages to reduce the range to a minimum.

(2) The teachers are given personal attention. Taught in small groups in a residential setting, a great deal of interest is shown in the individual's progress. Furthermore, the distance learning packs are 'personalised' to ensure that they meet the teacher's needs, and access to a tutor reduces the feelings of isolation that many learners feel in such situations and motivates the individual to meet the short-term goals, i.e. completion of a unit and the submission of the recording.

(3) The courses offer accreditation in the form of IoL and other qualifications, and teachers may also gain access to the Polytechnic Diploma or IoL via evening courses at Preston. Although many teachers will follow a course of study and neither require the external recognition for professional reasons nor want a further qualification for personal reasons, the number of teachers who do sit IoL and other examinations suggests that there is a motivating element in such accreditation. After all, tests, examinations and assessments are the currency of teaching. It may well be the case that teachers learning a new language or improving their competence in a language find that the newly acquired linguistic capability is not demonstrable in their daily work either because they do not teach the language or because the level at which they teach the language is much lower than the level of study and they consequently feel the need for more tangible proof of their achievements. It is worth noting that accreditation can also benefit the providers of funding, namely the LEAs and eventually also the individual schools under Local Management of Schools (LMS). It must be remembered that funding is a finite resource and that the allocation of grants has, increasingly, to be fought for and justified. There is a quantifiable element to the INSET that has been described and it may well strengthen the hand of the advisers/inspectors and heads of department if teachers are shown to be reaching particular levels of attainment as a result of their further study.

The final point is the importance of the methodology employed in the training. It was mentioned previously that the approach was communicative. The benefits of this are clear but are worth mentioning. Firstly, these methods most closely correspond to the needs of the teacher. Teachers requiring retraining identify the oral/aural skills as being by far the most important.[8] Teachers need to feel competent in using the target language in class in order to be confident, and they regard the pupils' respect for the teacher's professional ability to be an essential ingredient in the maintenance of discipline. Whereas with reading and writing the teacher has time to think and prepare a response, the other skills operate in 'real time' and do not allow for the same delay. Secondly, it is through such an approach that the culture of the country can best be presented. Exposure to as much input as possible through video, audio-tapes, native speakers and realia are all essential to the presentation of the culture (in addition to residence abroad, if possible). The cultural aspects assume great importance in the case of teachers who have spent little time in the country of the language they are learning or improving. Teachers need to be confident that they can fulfil the demands of the National Criteria in terms of cultural awareness and speak authoritatively about the customs of the country. Thirdly, by exposing the teachers to communicative methodology teachers are reminded what it is like to be a learner and the value of such an approach is reinforced. The courses offer a model of good practice and give teachers new ideas for the presentation of material, thereby fulfilling two INSET needs at once, the linguistic and the methodological.

Organisational needs

The organisational and methodological aspects have a great deal in common. First of all, they are likely to be overshadowed by the other type of INSET mentioned and are likely to be overlooked by both teachers and advisory staff. There is a real danger that modern language departments will simply 'stretch' their existing practices and materials to accommodate the expansion of their activities; courses designed for three years' study will simply be supplemented to last five years; teaching in the first three years of secondary school will remain the same, and measures to cope with the problems in the upper school will be superficial. Motivating pupils and satisfying the different needs of pupils of a wide range of ability over five years is very different from teaching a minority beyond the age of fourteen. Teachers need to spend time examining and discussing all aspects of their teaching and organisation before the introduction of the National Curriculum. To be made aware of all the issues and possibilities is an important function of INSET.

Coping with change requires organisation: planning and negotiating are the key areas in which teachers need to be strong. Ironically this is an area in which many have little experience and often no training. For many, planning is restricted to the needs of the academic year to come and negotiation is also an annual event linked to discussions about staff replacements, timetabling problems and capitation. Given the largely insular nature of life in the classroom and the lack of collaborative contact time with colleagues, it is not surprising that many teachers are ill-prepared for lengthy negotiations and planning.

That being said, it must be emphasised that if teachers are to get the best for their department and their pupils under the National Curriculum they will need to give a lot of attention to these areas and they can be helped here by INSET.

Teachers need to know first of all how to present their case – who to talk to, in what order to approach different interest groups, what can be achieved and agreed at each stage (cf. Figure 1). Heads of department who have sought and obtained permission to diversify or have fixed a date for a language in the core may feel that their negotiations are at an end. They will have discussed some of the issues below but there may well be others which need to be addressed:

(1) Staffing: increased staffing, staff offering different combinations of languages;
(2) Resources: new course materials, equipment, increased capitation;
(3) Room allocation: an extra teacher will need an extra room;
(4) Staff recognition: increased status for modern languages will mean more allowances;
(5) Timetabling for FL2: when, what, how and to whom?
(6) Timetabling provision: over five years, what about dual linguists?
(7) Provision post 16: in 11 to 18 schools;
(8) Setting, language allocation;
(9) PR: nature and scope of 'marketing';
(10) Visits and exchanges: timing, nature of visits, parity between FL1s;
(11) Use of assistants: increased provision, parity between FL1s;
(12) INSET provision.

In order to negotiate successfully there must be forward planning and research. Sadly, teachers are discouraged by their circumstances from planning ahead; falling rolls (sometimes resulting in redeployment and indiscriminate cuts in staffing), school closures, LMS (which will make LEA planning extremely difficult), opting out and tertiary reorganisation have led many schools to adopt a hand-to-mouth existence.

Nevertheless, schools in general, and modern language departments in particular, are going to have to make projections based on whatever information they have. It is clear that in the case of diversification and the National Curriculum the planning projections must be over at least five years, since it takes this long for the effects of the changes to work through the system. In order to make such projections teachers do not have to turn into timetabling or curricular deputy heads but they do need to be able to work out their staffing needs over such a period, and to be aware of timetabling constraints in general and, in particular, those related to a specific model of diversification. Such work does involve 'number crunching' but is not difficult, simply unfamiliar to many teachers. They need to be able to present a profile of their modern language staffing and timetabling commitments (such as the mapping instrument prepared by John Marshall HMI[9]) and to present their staffing projections clearly, highlighting the factors behind the figures. It may well be that a number of projections have to be made based on different possibilities.

The effects on others of a well-prepared argument are predictable but need to be stressed.

(1) It puts the case effectively and convincingly and does not waste time.

(2) It increases the status and respect of the head of department in the eyes of his/her superiors.

(3) It is likely to produce a certain empathy between the head/deputy and the head of department, since the latter will have had to consider and cope with some of the same problems as the deputy has to face right across the curriculum and so is likely to be more sympathetic as a result.

Negotiations are not restricted to heads and deputies of course, as we can see from the diagram below. First of all the modern language department has to be consulted and kept informed of developments; other staff have to be told especially when and if they are directly affected by the changes; governors need to be informed; parents of prospective pupils and the pupils themselves need to have the ideas presented to them. In other words the head of department needs to be adept public relations.

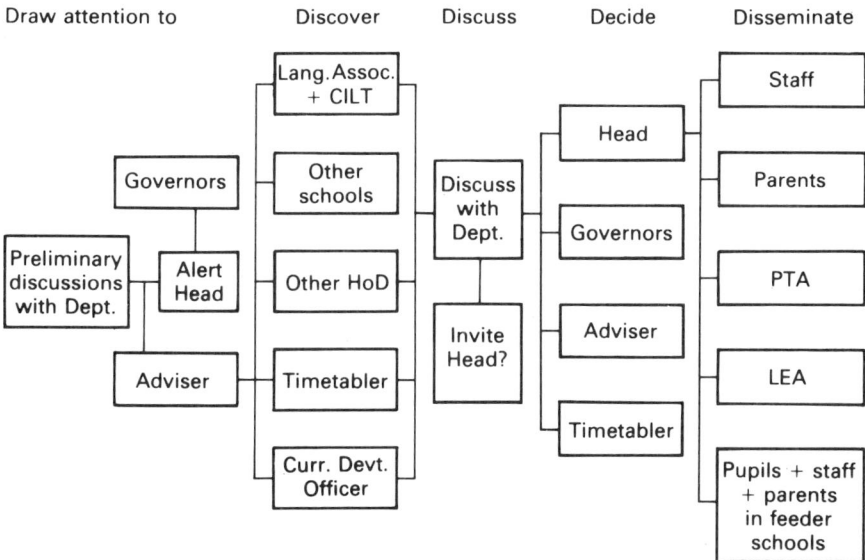

Draw attention to		Discover	Discuss	Decide	Disseminate
		Lang. Assoc. + CILT			Staff
				Head	
Governors		Other schools	Discuss with Dept.		Parents
Preliminary discussions with Dept.	Alert Head	Other HoD		Governors	PTA
			Invite Head?	Adviser	LEA
Adviser		Timetabler			
				Timetabler	
		Curr. Devt. Officer			Pupils + staff + parents in feeder schools

Research was mentioned earlier as a negotiating tool. Teachers need to be armed with evidence from a variety of sources in order to help to convince others. Examples of good practice and successful implementation of change in other schools, statistics and documentary evidence to support arguments, all add weight to the case. Teachers need to know whom to ask. With so much change taking place in a short time and so much information available, teachers need help in facing the challenge of keeping abreast with the latest reports and developments and they need too to be reminded of the support and facilities available from organisations such as CILT (Centre for Information on Language Teaching and Research), CBEVE (Central Bureau for Educational Visits and Exchanges) and ALL (Association for Language Learning).

Michael Calvert

Methodological needs

The planning must take into account the methodological implications. Teaching a five-year course to pupils of all abilities does not simply call for a modification of the existing provision but a total rethink. As was previously stated, there is a real danger that this will not be appreciated and that existing materials in the original FL1 will simply be 'stretched' to accommodate all pupils and that, in the case of the new FL1 (promoted from FL2), the teachers will underestimate the problems of the changes. There are important differences between teaching a minority of pupils who have opted to take the subject over a shorter period of time from that of the FL1 and using materials designed for FL2 use, and teaching 11 year old beginners with no foreign language experience.

What is required is a complete reappraisal of all aspects of methodology: materials used; levels of attainment at different stages; a policy on assessment; and an evaluation of different assessment techniques, both formative and summative.

Teachers must be aware of the need to produce a flexible course which caters for the needs of all ages and abilities. Pacing, sequencing and differentiation are key factors in deciding what to teach, when and how. If the pupils are not successful and motivated in the early years, and if their motivation and interest cannot be sustained over a five-year period, there may well be serious problems in the classroom. The teacher needs to have clear objectives (short, medium and long-term) which are understood and shared by the pupils; the pupils need to achieve the goals set and to enjoy the satisfaction of succeeding, and both they and their parents need to be kept informed; the grading of work needs to be such that no pupil is faced with a task that is too difficult, and all pupils need to be given a great deal of varied practice and revision throughout; pupils need to be challenged and intellectually stimulated from the start, and this should continue throughout the five years.

Once the course has been mapped out and a scheme of work established by the department, the head of department has to make sure that the teachers are all working in similar ways to achieve the goals set. It is not the case that new examinations, new materials or changing situations necessarily influence a teacher's methodological approach. Teachers preparing pupils for GOML (Graded Objectives in Modern Languages) tests by presenting the pupils with vocabulary and phrase lists to learn for the test is just one example of inappropriate methodology.

We face a situation in which the teaching for GCSE does make new demands on teachers; more pair work and group work are a consequence of the greater emphasis on oral/aural work and the nature of the language tasks presented; there is a need for much more authentic material and corresponding authentic tasks; there needs to be a greater understanding of the relationship between the teaching of grammar and the communicative needs of the learner. Add to this the demands likely to be made by the increased range of ability and the need for more individualised attention, and it is evident that some teachers are going to need a lot of help and support. If the teachers are not given the training and do not understand the ideas underlying the new communicative courses there could be a serious mismatch between:

(a) the materials and the methodology, and
(b) the teaching styles of the different members of department.

Having looked at the organisational and methodological needs of teachers, it is necessary now to look at ways of helping them through INSET. One of the features of the linguistic INSET suggested was the need for flexibility. This is also the case here. There is a need for INSET materials which cater for teachers with varying amounts of experience and different outlooks, in a variety of situations: 'Baker days', INSET courses and self-study.

The material needs to be practical and relevant. Work on negotiating, for example, might involve prioritising the issues to be discussed, preparing one's case, observing others negotiating (on video) and similation exercises in pairs, the partner playing the role of headteacher. Teachers will also need to spend time discussing the issues raised and working things out together.

It is valuable if examples can be presented which offer a model of successful practice. These can be used both as illustrations for the purposes of the course and if, in the case of diversification, it were possible to show examples to headteachers and others it could strengthen the hand of the head of department.

Such material has been developed at the University of York in the form of a handbook and video. The handbook contains discussion material, workshop activities and notes on how the material can be used. The video contains examples of German, Italian, Russian and Spanish in Year 1 and interviews with the teacher and pupils in each case. It also shows two interviews between a headteacher and a head of department to illustrate the need for preparation and good negotiating skills.

Conclusion

All the INSET described above relies on two things: funding and resources, both human and material. Ideally each LEA requires teachers' centres geographically well-situated, resource centres with all the most recent courses available on loan, and a comprehensive policy on training and retraining of teachers. Even in LEAs which have all three there is often insufficient manpower (or expertise) to satisfy all the INSET needs. LEA advisers are taking on a much more inspectorial role and there are often insufficient advisory teachers to meet the training needs.

In the case of Lancashire, it would be easy to say that the authority is extremely fortunate in having a number of colleges 'on the doorstep'. It is true to say that not all authorities are as fortunate. Many LEAs, however, could call upon the services of local institutions to satisfy some or all of their INSET needs. There is clearly going to have to be greater cooperation between LEAs and universities/colleges if the INSET needs described are to be met. A symbiotic relationship between the two would be extremely beneficial; the LEAs could tap the colleges' expertise and the colleges could find a ready market for their services.

If such schemes are to work throughout the country there is a pressing need to coordinate the efforts of the different institutions by means of regional/national cooperation. The DES policy statement[10] calls for 'concerted and vigorous action . . . needed from LEAs, school teachers and teacher trainers to bring about the necessary changes'. However, there is a marked lack of policy in the recent documents (DES 1987,[11] 1988) concerning the balance of languages in the National Curriculum. Priority treatment should be given to languages such as Italian, Russian, and Spanish so that these languages are more evenly represented throughout the country. It is difficult to see the role that the LEAs are going to be able to play in such matters as INSET when, with the advent of LMS, their influence declines and the funding is in the hands of the schools. What coordinated INSET contribution could they then make?

Whatever happens, the next five to ten years will be crucial for the teaching of modern languages. The future of languages other than French is at stake; the credibility of a policy of teaching a language to all abilities is in doubt; and the guarantee of a supply of good linguists into the teaching profession is far from secure. It is essential that modern language teachers be well prepared for the task in hand.

10

Diversification and the National Curriculum: Policy and Provision

Georgina Clark

In February 1988 the Department of Education and Science (DES) and the Welsh Office issued the long-awaited document *Modern Languages in the School Curriculum: A Statement of Policy*.[1] It addressed the place of modern foreign language teaching in the curriculum of pupils at various stages of their school education, the range of languages which should be available in schools, and the nature and quality of the provision. Its publication marked a major new departure in the teaching of modern languages in schools. For the first time policy decisions made by central government were issued in published form with the implication that they be implemented throughout England and Wales. In order to comply with these new national policies LEAs, governing bodies, headteachers and teachers are now called upon to adopt policies for foreign language teaching in schools which give direct expression to the principles set out in the statement.

Modern Languages in the School Curriculum sets three targets for development by LEAs and schools. The first concerns the availability and take-up of languages and requires that at least one foreign language be studied as part of the common curriculum up to the age of sixteen. Schools are also required to set targets for increased take-up of languages among sixth form pupils. The second requirement for schools and LEAs is to improve standards of communication in pupils of all abilities. Thirdly, and of particular interest here, *Modern Languages in the School Curriculum* calls for greater diversification of first foreign language provision.

Policy, as Fenwick and McBride have pointed out, represents a 'usually slow development of thinking that is gradually translated into commitment',[2] a process which frequently involves a long gestation period. Policy, however, as the same authors acknowledge, may also spring from *ad hoc* decisions by the Minister or Secretary of State, which represent not the product of educational or political thinking over a prolonged period, but rather a response to immediate political pressure or current economic conditions. The Government's policy statement on modern languages shows elements of both of these strands of development.

Immediate precursors to the February statement took the form of two similarly named documents issued by the DES, *Foreign Languages in the School Curriculum: A Consultative Paper*[3] and *Foreign Languages in the School Curriculum: A Draft Statement of Policy*.[4] These in turn were influenced by a number of reports highlighting issues relating to the provision of language teaching in schools produced by the Assessment of Performance Unit[5] and two documents from the Schools Council[6] which concentrated on the position of second languages in the curriculum. HMI recommendations were also contributory factors.[7] Further key areas of discussion prior to the issue of the 1988 policy statement focussed more generally on the development of the National Curriculum, which was to have profound implications for the teaching of modern languages in schools.

In terms of the National Curriculum, a modern foreign language is designated a Foundation Subject to be taught to all pupils in key stages 4 and 5 of compulsory schooling, that is from age 11 to 16. This will entail massive changes in the nation's schools where currently (1989) only about 34% of pupils continue the study of a language, usually French, into the option Years 4 and 5. In particular, the inclusion of a compulsory foreign language element in the common curriculum of all pupils has significant effects on the study of second languages, and by implication, since it is in the area of second language study that scope has traditionally been given to languages other than French, on the issue of diversification.

An important early indication of the effects of the inclusion of a compulsory language element in the National Curriculum was supplied by the HMI study with the unwieldy title *An inquiry into practice in 22 comprehensive schools where a foreign language forms part of the curriculum for all or almost all pupils to age 16*, more commonly referred to as *The 22 Schools*.[8] This revealed that in such schools, time available to optional studies was significantly curtailed, with the result that 'the second language faces much more competition and the proportion of pupils taking it is likely to be reduced'.[9]

> The major factor affecting the second foreign language in the fourth year would appear to be the proportion of time given to the core curriculum; the more extensive the core, the lower the take-up is likely to be for a second foreign language, all other factors being equal. If the number of pupils taking a language other than French is to be maintained, let alone increased, then the most likely way forward would seem to be to offer these languages more frequently as first or equal first languages.

The 22 Schools also showed what many teachers instinctively feel, namely that compulsory subjects are in general less popular with pupils than subjects which they can choose themselves. Popularity, furthermore, was seen to be related to the perceived difficulties of a subject, with French considered by average pupils as the most difficult of all compulsory subjects, and with noticeable differences in difficulty perceived by boys compared to girls. These findings were further supported by studies conducted by the Assessment of Performance Unit and discussed in this volume by Caroline Filmer-Sankey. Together they raised important questions on the viability and the relative appeal of languages other than French.

For many years before the APU survey of 1983 suggested that some pupils respond more positively to languages other than French as first foreign language, educators and professional bodies interested in the field of modern language teaching had been arguing against what was seen as the hegemony of French in British schools. As early as 1918, when the Leathes Report[10] was seeking to extend provision for 'modern studies' in schools and universities, there was some dissent against the notion that French, as the Leathes Report put it, was 'among living languages ... beyond question the ... most important'. Whereas this sentence was widely quoted to justify the high profile of French in British schools, subsequent sections of the report were largely ignored. It continued:

> But it is not necessary that the first living language should be French in all schools. There may be districts and there may be schools in which German or even Spanish or Italian may be preferable.[11]

Indeed, three members of the committee which produced the Leathes Report declined to sign the paragraphs advocating French as first foreign language. They wrote in an appendix:

> We think ... that there would be a great loss if ... the work of a considerable proportion of the pupils was limited to a single language, especially as it is obvious that for the large majority the first, and often the only language learned, would be French. It seems to us that French does not and cannot by itself provide all that is necessary for language training.[12]

The dissenters went on:

> We do not hold that French is the language best suited to discipline and train the youthful mind to an appreciation of language and its use. If it is to be the first language learned, it requires supplementing by a second language, and it should not be taken for granted that a child who makes no progress in French is for that same reason alone incapable of acquiring any foreign language. We were informed by some of our witnesses that certain children were able to succeed with Latin or German although they had failed with French.[13]

Given that in so many schools languages other than French have been offered only to those deemed successful in French, it is a great pity that the recommendations of the Leathes Report in large measure remained unobserved. However, theirs was by no means the only plea for diversification to fall on deaf ears before the implications of the National Curriculum for the provision of modern languages made diversification politic.

Already in the mid-1970s, the Modern Languages Committee of the Schools Council had become concerned about the position of languages other than French in secondary schools. A working party, set up in 1975, then reached the conclusion that the only way in which any impact could be made against the predominance of French would be for more schools to introduce German, Spanish or other languages as *first* rather than as *second* foreign language taught within a school. Having been made aware of the difficulties which schools felt they would face if they attempted to replace French as first foreign language, the Committee soon realised that there was a great lack of reliable information available to schools on the question of diversification, and beginning in the late summer of 1979, set about the task of trying to provide schools with that information. With falling rolls threatening languages other than French, speed was deemed to be of the essence. In April 1981 they produced, therefore, not a full-scale project, but a shorter study, *Languages other than French in the secondary school: an exploratory study of other languages as first or equal first foreign language.*[14] In Chapter One, outlining the background to the study (which has become widely known as the Hadley Report) the authors explained:

> It is because languages other than French are commonly the second language and because the second language is in some peril that the idea of diversification of the first language has been promoted.[15]

A questionnaire was devised to produce from schools offering a language other than French as first or equal first foreign language, information on staffing, the organisation of the subject, the reasons for adopting the language, parental reactions and so on. In addition 23 schools were selected for detailed study before the questionnaires were despatched. The working group wished to examine schools of different sizes, schools in different urban or rural contexts, schools in very different parts of the country, schools offering a sole first language and those offering more than one first language either equally or unequally, and either concurrently or in alternate years. The conclusions which this exploratory study reached, in summary, were as follows:

(1) There is nothing in the nature of a language other than French which makes it either more or less feasible than French as a first foreign language in secondary schools.[16]

(2) There is a good degree of favour for the notion of diversification of first foreign languages among local authorities, but few have a definite, clearly perceived policy for modern language teaching in their schools.[17]

(3) Parents exercise little or no influence on a school's language policy, but have a strong feeling that French should be available at some point.

(4) External influences play a minimal role in a school's decision about which first language to offer. The decision depends rather on the enthusiasm and commitment of the staff.

(5) Sympathetic timetabling is essential, particularly with regard to option

grouping, and capable linguists should not be allowed to opt out.

(6) In making decisions on which language or languages to offer, schools should bear in mind that the numerical base for a language in the first year of a course bears a distinct relationship to its later viability. A comprehensive school with an ideal distribution of ability needs at least eight forms of entry to run two languages.

(7) Which of the languages to offer other than French depends almost entirely upon the enthusiasm, preference and circumstances of the school.

(8) French should figure in a school's curriculum as a safeguard against potential criticism and to aid transfers-in. On this point, where French is offered as a joint first language, it should not initially be filled to capacity. Where French is the second language it is advantageous for it to be begun in the second year.[18]

(9) The problem of transfers-in may not be being fully faced, although some schools absorb late entrants for a new language through specially prepared cassette tapes and worksheets.

(10) Staffing has not shown itself to be more difficult for languages other than French but with the present levels of teacher supply this situation would change if there were more than a limited expansion of these languages as first language.

(11) Where two first languages are offered, the second language tends to be weak.

(12) With norm referencing in public examinations, there is a general feeling that it is more difficult for candidates to achieve a good grade in languages other than French.[19]

(13) The value of support services, in particular the presence of a foreign language assistant, was evident.

(14) There was a conviction that sixth-form examinations should be reformed.

(15) There is a wide variety of practice in a decentralised education system. The health of modern languages would be better if there were a greater degree of direction and cooperation.

Following the publication of the Hadley Report, in the autumn of 1982 the Assessment of Performance Unit conducted a survey to ascertain how many schools were teaching languages other than French as first foreign languages, and with what results. As information received from LEAs revealed that their records of provision would not be sufficiently precise to supply these data, a questionnaire was sent to all schools in England which, on the basis of LEA data, were expected to be teaching German or Spanish as first foreign language, and to a stratified random sample of the remaining schools in England, Wales and Northern Ireland. Some 1,049 questionnaires were returned and analysed to produce a report entitled *Foreign Language Provision*.[20] In it 90% of schools were reported as teaching French as first foreign language but only 21% German, and a meagre 4% Spanish. More worrying still, eleven schools were teaching none of these, in most cases because no foreign language was being offered at all. Reorganisation of schools, moreover, falling rolls, and shortage and change of staff were shown to be having wide-ranging effects on modern languages provision, as the following comments culled from the report indicate:

(1) with falling rolls French had to be discontinued, but will be taught again to CSE level when several small secondary schools amalgamate into one comprehensive school;

(2) possibility of closure means staffing problems, and, therefore, some children get no French at all;

(3) the change from selective to comprehensive means that we can no longer offer French, German, Spanish and Russian from the first year; all pupils will learn French;

(4) at present, French and German are taught from entry; next year's smaller intake will learn French only;

(5) a second language added in year 2 has been discontinued;

(6) Italian can no longer be taught;

(7) Spanish teacher cannot be replaced.

There were some instances where staff changes, changes in school policy, and experiments and innovations had broadened the extent and variety of language teaching, but these comments were indicative of the problems faced by schools experiencing falling rolls and the potentially detrimental effects these could have on language provision nationally.

The advisers to the Secretaries of State for Education cannot have been blind to the precarious position of languages other than French in the nation's schools. Already in 1981 the Education, Science and Arts Committee had warned the House of Commons:

> So far as the minority languages are concerned, we are convinced from the evidence before us that there is a real danger that unless some positive action is taken many of these are in danger of disappearing altogether, and that those that are not are likely to become rare offerings in our schools.[21]

Then, in the spring of 1982 the Schools Council produced the ominously titled *The Second Foreign Language in Secondary Schools: a question of survival*, which made it clear that the position of the second foreign language had been affected by two compounding trends, the first being the failure of modern languages to maintain their share of a growing market in the middle and upper part of secondary schools, the second being the continued imbalance between French and other languages. The report stated:

> The second foreign language has not benefited as one might have expected from the years of expansion and affluence in secondary education: in many schools, and not merely at sixth form level, the second language would fail any reasonable test of cost effectiveness.

If pedagogical reasons for introducing languages other than French as first foreign language went largely unheeded, economic arguments and the repeatedly voiced risk of depleting still further the number of pupils emerging from secondary schools with a qualification in a language other than French did not. The findings of the Hadley Report were cited in the DES/Welsh Office publication of 1983, *Foreign Languages in the School Curriculum: A Consultative Paper*, to which reference has already been made. This contained a number of references to the imbalance between the teaching of French and that of other languages in secondary schools, an imbalance which the DES thought it necessary to rectify in the interests of national trade and cultural relations. Paragraph 31 stated:

> Our links with other European countries make it desirable to study the language and culture of as many of them as is practicable. Industry and commerce need a strong capability in a number of languages, both in their general and their specialist staff, and this needs as wide a base of successful language as it is practicable for the schools to provide.

The issue of practicability, was of course, crucial, and it was at this point that the calls for diversification were finally heeded by the policy makers in the DES. Paragraph 32 opened: 'However, if languages other than French are to survive, let alone flourish, at school level, they need to be much more frequently offered as the first foreign language.' Henceforward the introduction of diversification of first foreign languages became one of the major focusses of DES policy for modern language teaching.

When the Secretaries of State were drawing up new national policies on language provision, from the consultation document *Foreign Languages in the School Curriculum* of 1983 to the definitive policy statement *Modern Languages in the Curriculum* of 1988, 1992 and its new trading agreements were already looming, with consequent implications for national resources in linguistic competence. Diversification of first foreign language provision was by now essential if the United Kingdom was not to fall rapidly out of step with the rest of Europe. Much of the thinking which the 1988 policy statement contained was already evident in the earlier consultation document of 1983. However, over those five years, subtle, but significant changes were introduced as far as the question of diversification was concerned, in particular affecting the pace and resourcing of proposed changes. The consultation paper put forward but tentative proposals for diversification and conceded that:

> in any case the scope for diversification of provision is limited by the capacity of the

existing teaching force, the cost incurred in utilising that capacity differently and the willingness of teachers, pupils, parents and LEAs to adapt.[22]

In terms of costs, 'the economical use of teaching expertise' was deemed to be vital, because, as the consultative paper made clear under the heading 'constraints on change' (paragraphs 55 to 58), it was:

> unrealistic to expect that new resources [would] be immediately available to the schools for the improvement of foreign language teaching on the scale . . . of the 1960s or early 1970s so as to extend the scale of foreign language provision.

The supply of teachers necessary to implement proposals for extending the provision and take-up of modern languages was not thought to be a problem, however. Paragraph 56 opened with the confident statement: 'The supply of foreign language teachers has improved and it seems likely that most of the comparatively few vacancies arising in schools will readily be filled.' Drawing on figures from the Secondary School Staffing Survey of 1977, paragraph 57 added: 'the evidence suggests that there may be a reserve of teachers able to provide teaching in a wider range of languages than is now the case'.[23] Paragraph 59 also proposed that teachers without formal qualifications in a foreign language 'nevertheless know it sufficiently well to make a valuable contribution to teaching it, especially in oral and conversational work'.[24]

The authors of the consultative paper thus clearly ignored, or were ignorant of, the warning of 'severe difficulties in staffing' modern languages made by the Education, Science and Arts Committee in 1981.[25] They did acknowledge, however, that because of limitations on financial resources 'it is likely that the pattern of provision, particularly the diversification of the languages taught, can be developed only gradually.'

In June 1986, the issues put forward in the consultative document were then redrafted in the form of the DES/Welsh Office publication *Foreign Languages in the School Curriculum: A Draft Statement of Policy*. This draft policy statement set the learning of languages firmly in the context of national requirements:

> The Government's policies for schools – set out in the White Paper 'Better Schools' – are founded on the belief that education at school can and should have lasting and beneficial effects on the prosperity and well-being of individuals and of the nation. Worthwhile skills in foreign languages are a lasting asset which can be developed and put to use by people at work or in their personal lives at home and abroad. It is not only the individuals concerned who benefit from being able to communicate with foreigners in their own language. The country too can benefit economically and culturally: opportunities will be opened up in trade, tourism, international relations, science and other fields. The development of such opportunities can make a practical contribution to improving Britain's effectiveness as a member of the European Community.[26]

Many schools, it was recognised, offered German, Spanish or Italian as a second foreign language, but the number of pupils who took them was noted to be small. To increase the uptake of languages other than French it was proposed that some larger schools offering only French as the first foreign language should consider offering two first foreign languages, and that smaller schools might break altogether with the tradition of French, and offer some other language in its place, with French as second language. It was acknowledged that this might mean that pupils changing schools would not be able to depend on continuity of language studies, but paragraph 38 of the report suggested that 'if enough schools offer a range of languages and if LEAs and schools are ready to respond positively to pupils' needs, adverse effects should be minimised'. On the issue of diversification, paragraph 43 concluded:

> The need for diversification is pressing. However, constraints on resources will, to some extent, affect how quickly it can be brought about. The costs of preparing schools and teachers to offer a different or alternative first foreign language will present the education service with difficult decisions about priorities. However, a short term redirection of existing resources, together with careful planning, would enable authorities to tap a resource which is at present wasted. The result nationally would be a richer and more motivating experience for young people and a curriculum better suited to the country's needs.

Much of the rest of the draft policy statement focussed on the desire to improve standards in modern languages, citing the results of the APU surveys of 1983 and 1984 in support of its arguments. Paragraph 71 concluded:

> We recognise that some – but by no means all – of the necessary developments will require extra resources, and that the pace of change will depend on the rate at which those resources can be made available. We believe however that much can be done in present circumstances through a recognition of the importance of foreign languages and a determination to make a start on reshaping provision.

The draft policy statement of 1986 thus acknowledged that in order to implement changes, investment of both time and money would be necessary. The pace at which diversification could be introduced would depend upon constraints on resources. The goal of a language for all remained a goal and not a statutory requirement, involving a minimum of three years from the beginning of the secondary phase and not compulsory throughout secondary schooling. A second language was also to be offered, possibly from Years 3 or 2 if curricular time could be made available, and, importantly, it was acknowledged that widening the provision of language teaching would call for additional spending in relation to planning, the training of teachers and the acquisition of new materials.

By the time that the Government was ready to release the definitive *Modern Languages in the School Curriculum: a Statement of Policy*, the Education Reform Bill introducing the new National Curriculum had been read in Parliament. *Modern Languages in the School Curriculum* now made it clear that: 'The Government's proposals for the National Curriculum are that a modern foreign language should be a foundation subject studied by all pupils throughout compulsory schooling'. In anticipation of the passing of the Education Reform Act, paragraph 20 stressed that:

> LEAs and schools should take steps now to make continuation of a modern foreign

language one of the compulsory elements of the 14–16 curriculum for the great majority of pupils.

On the question of diversification, addressed in paragraphs 30 to 40, the DES made it clear under paragraph 32 that:

> LEAs and schools should ensure that a reasonable proportion of their pupils of all abilities should study a language other than French as their first foreign language . . . ,

adding: 'On commercial and cultural grounds, priority should be given to the main languages of the European Community'.[27]

As in the draft policy statement, it was again suggested that in order to implement this, larger schools should offer two alternative foreign languages whilst smaller schools might offer a language other than French as first foreign language, retaining French as a second language option. In spite of the fact that twenty months had intervened between the publication of the draft policy statement and the definitive policy statement, their wording was virtually identical. There were, however, a limited number of significant shifts of emphasis.

Firstly, and of considerable import as far as the range of language provision was concerned, whereas the draft policy statement still retained the notion of introducing a second foreign language for some pupils from Years 2 or 3, the definitive policy statement maintained that this would be 'inconsistent with the central aim of achieving a broad and balanced curriculum in those years'. Secondly, on the issue of diversification, whereas the draft policy statement had simply referred to the dominance of French in secondary schools as 'inappropriate to the needs of a modern trading nation', the definitive statement made it plain that 'this position is not satisfactory'. Furthermore, whilst the draft policy statement suggested that 'some larger schools . . . should consider offering two first foreign languages', the definitive statement urged that 'in order to secure diversification, larger schools should . . . offer two alternative first foreign languages', the omission of the words 'some' and 'consider' lending much greater weight to the Government's drive towards diversification of first foreign language provision. However, reference to the costs of implementing this policy was cut. Whereas the draft policy statement acknowledged that 'the costs of preparing schools and teachers to offer a different or alternative first foreign language will present the education service with difficult decisions about priorities', in the definitive policy statement this sentence appeared with the words 'the costs of' omitted, significantly altering its import. Finally, the opening statement of the concluding paragraph of the definitive policy document was amended from the draft form:

> we recognise that some – but by no means all – of the necessary developments will require extra resources, and that the pace of change will depend on the rate at which these extra resources can be made available

to:

> we expect that the resources currently devoted to local policies for modern foreign

language teaching will be directed in support of the policies outlined in this statement.

The definitive Government policy statement of February 1988 was thus considerably more demanding of schools and LEAs than the preceding draft, whilst at the same time indicating that all necessary changes had to be made within existing resources. LEAs are now faced with the difficult problem of how to implement these changes in order to comply with DES policies.

The relationship between local education authorities and central government has never been an easy one. Ever since the Government first recognised a degree of responsibility for education in 1833 with the first state grants to voluntary schools, local providers of education have strenuously defended their right to determine the purpose and nature of their schools. With the passing of the 1944 Education Act, a complex web of interdependent relationships was formally established between the Minister or Secretary of State responsible for education and the county or county borough councils. In practice, however, in the 1950s and 1960s the balance of power in matters of educational provision progressively shifted away from central government towards the LEAs.[28] Since the 1970s successive Secretaries of State have moved to arrest the decline in influence of the DES and to reassert control over the curriculum and national provision.

In November 1977, governmental concern over the autonomy of LEAs in matters relating to the curriculum resulted in the issue of DES Circular 14/77, designed to elicit detailed information about curriculum arrangements in each of the then 105 local education authorities, so as to provide central government with an overview of national provision. The report resulting from Circular 14/77, published as *Local Authority Arrangements for the School Curriculum* in November 1979, revealed substantial variations within the educational system in England and Wales in terms of policies concerning the curriculum. Interpretation of the word 'policy', furthermore, was revealed to be extremely wide, ranging from detailed written statements produced centrally within certain authorities to a much less formal arrangement of providing encouragement and support to initiatives and practices arising in individual schools.

As far as the question of which languages were to be taught in the secondary sector was concerned, two-fifths of responses indicated that the authority had not formulated a specific policy on this issue. However, several authorities reported that their advisers were concerned to encourage schools to broaden the provision of modern languages, for example by offering French and German in alternate years as first language or by appointing non-French specialists as heads of department. Only a few authorities said that they required all secondary schools to offer French as the first modern language; a quarter, however, said that, while they had not made this a requirement, in practice all schools did offer French as the first modern language, while a further two-fifths said that this was the case in the majority of schools.

Concerned at this apparent lack of guidance from LEAs and at the wide discrepancies between authorities evident from these findings, the authors of the report advised 'the task now is to see what conclusions can be drawn that will lead to a more coherent approach in curricular matters across the country'. The report argued:

> There is a need for clear policies on the provision of modern languages in primary, middle and secondary schools. Such policies must take account of the availability of teachers. The dominant position of French gives rise to concern about the position of other major languages. Decisions about the ages at which children should start (and finish) modern language courses, and about the languages available, are often made at school level. The Secretaries of State believe that there should be more local coordination in the light of broad guidelines which would help to promote national coherence and protect the position of less commonly taught modern languages.[29]

In January 1980, two months after the appearance of *Local Authority Arrangements for the School Curriculum*, the DES issued *A Framework for the Curriculum*, paragraph four of which reiterated that 'the Secretaries of State consider that each education authority should have a clear and known policy for the curriculum offered in its schools'. Addressing specifically the issue of modern languages, *A Framework for the Curriculum* pointed out:

> While most secondary schools offer French as their first (or only) modern language, and it would not be practicable or desirable to change this, it is important that other languages should be widely available, and available as first modern language for some pupils. Local authorities should keep under review the provision made for modern languages in their schools, and seek to ensure an adequate variety of languages in each area.

The Hadley Report of 1981, however, revealed that the majority of schools it surveyed felt they received little guidance on these matters from their respective LEAs. From an analysis of responses to the question 'Has your local education authority a policy for modern languages? If yes, what is your perception of it?', put to schools as part of its investigation begun in the late summer of 1979, the authors concluded that most schools believed that their local authority had *no* policy for modern languages. Indeed, only four out of 22 responses (representing nineteen LEAs) answered this question in the affirmative. However, whereas the majority of schools stated that the authority did *not* have a policy, the majority of LEAs, when interviewed, said that they *did*. The Hadley Report concluded:

> This paradox summarises the present state of school/local education authority relationships. Unless authorities are able to implement curricular planning, schools may pursue their own initiatives or discount central advice.

Henceforward calls for LEAs to monitor and coordinate provision in their schools and to develop clear policies for modern languages were frequently reiterated. Thus *The School Curriculum* of March 1981 exhorted:

> The Secretaries of State consider that the available language teaching resources can be used to full effect, and the best balance achieved between languages on offer, only if modern languages provision as a whole is planned by the local education authority across its area, taking account of the facilities available in both schools and further education.

As far as diversification was concerned the DES conceded:

> We do not underestimate the extent of planning required in LEAs and schools to bring about the diversification which is necessary. LEAs will need to know, or find out, what expertise in different languages exists within their teaching force, where it lies and how, if at all, it is being used at present. They will need to consider what training (in this country or abroad) is necessary to refresh teachers' competence in languages which they are not currently teaching; and whether their advisory services are adequate to support a policy of diversification. Once LEAs have assessed the potential expertise in various languages in their areas, they will need to draw up and put into action plans for deploying that expertise so as to increase the availability of languages other than French as first foreign languages. Looking to the longer term, authorities may need to review their recruitment objectives.[30]

In 1988 ten LEAs, selected on the basis of geographical distribution, language strengths, size and type of community and schools, and commitment to diversification, were awarded Educational Support Grants (ESGs) to finance pilot projects in order to implement these proposals. At the time of writing (May 1989) these projects have still to be evaluated.[31] However, in order to investigate how the remaining LEAs in England and Wales were responding to DES calls to widen the provision of languages other than French, in October 1988 OXPROD contacted all 98 authorities not involved in the DES-funded pilot scheme and invited them to respond to the following questions:

> Do you hold any information on the current provision for languages other than French in the authority?

> Do you have any plans to diversify first foreign language teaching in your schools?

A third question requested the name of anyone else in the authority to whom further enquiries on language provision and diversification should be addressed.

From the 41 replies received, representing authorities widely distributed over England and including two from Wales, it was clear that, as had been the case in 1977, there were vast discrepancies in both policy and provision in the different LEAs. Response towards diversification varied considerably, and was particularly cool, as might be expected, from areas with middle schools in which provision for languages other than French is understandably limited.[32] Perhaps the least enthusiastic reply was one which opened:

> Diversification: Modern Languages
> The answers are:
> (1) *oui*
> (2) *nein*
> (3) *niet*

This particular adviser expanded:

> It may be of interest to your research to note the bilious view of the ESG project taken in an area which is three-tier in its entirety with FL1 necessarily beginning in the 9 to

13 institutions. For a variety of reasons, therefore, diversification assumes – for me at least – some hollowness.

Elsewhere support for diversification was encouraging. In response to the question 'Do you have any plans to diversify first foreign language teaching in your schools', only the authority with the 'bilious view' cited above held a vehemently negative view of diversification. By contrast one authority was able to report 'six schools already offering a language other than French as first foreign language. A few more have plans for September 1989 (all German)', whilst another reported 'six schools out of 22 now offer German or Spanish as first or joint foreign language. It is hoped that there will be some increase in this number'. A third authority, which had applied unsuccessfully for ESG funding to support its plans for diversification, informed us:

> About ten schools have already adopted a policy of offering French and German on an equal footing to all (or nearly all) pupils on entry at 12+. The formula is usually three periods French plus three periods German (×35 minutes) over Years 2 and 3 to provide an *informed* choice to pupils in Year 3 when opting for one FL or two in Years 4 and 5. Since the issue of the DES Policy document in the Spring [of 1988] several schools have decided to diversify either from September 1988 or September 1989 – one school proposes to offer French, German and Spanish from Year 2. Others will bring either Spanish or German up to equal status with French

As David Phillips points out in the Introduction, other research conducted as part of OXPROD shows that many schools are already taking positive steps towards diversification of first language provision. Some, indeed, have been successfully offering languages other than French to their incoming pupils for many years. The challenge put to schools and LEAs by the current enthusiasm of the DES for diversification is, therefore, in some measure already being met. As other contributors to this volume reveal, the case for diversification is strong. Problems will have to be faced, not least in the supply and retraining of teachers, and in ensuring coordination of provision across and between LEAs, but we hope this volume will encourage both teachers and learners of modern languages to welcome the prospect of diversification.

References and Notes

Introduction

1 D Phillips: 'From Complacency to Conviction: thirty years of language teaching theory, practice and policy', in: *Languages in Schools*, ed. D Phillips, London, 1988 (CILT)
2 Assessment of Performance Unit (APU): *Foreign Language Performance in Schools. Report on 1983 survey of French, German and Spanish*, p. 391, London, 1985 (DES etc.)
3 DES: *DES News*, 31.1.89
4 D Phillips and G Clark: *Attitudes towards Diversification. Results of a survey of teacher opinion*, OXPROD Occasional Paper 1, p. 261, Oxford, 1988 (University of Oxford Department of Educational Studies)
5 F Rees: *Languages for a Change*, Windsor, 1989 (NFER-Nelson)
6 DES/Welsh Office: *Modern Languages in the School Curriculum: A Statement of Policy*, London, 1988 (HMSO)

The quotations interspersed throughout this Introduction are taken from the following sources:

a Schools Council: *Languages other than French in the secondary school: an exploratory study of other languages as first or equal first language* (Hadley Report), 1981
b DES: *Modern Languages in Comprehensive Schools*, HMI Series: Matters for Discussion 3, 1977 (HMSO)
c D Phillips and V Stencel: *The Second Foreign Language*, 1983 (Hodder and Stoughton)
d Scottish Education Department: *Alternatives to French as a first foreign language in secondary schools*, 1971
e E Allison Peers: *Spanish Now*, 1944 (Methuen)
f W H D Rowse: letter to *Modern Language Teaching*, November 1914
g R H Bird, Deputy Secretary at the DES, speech at a conference on oral and aural skills in the modern languages degree, Bradford University, 3.1.84
h Angela Rumbold speaking at the JCLA Conference, March 1987
i *The Teaching of Russian* (Annan Report) 1962 (HMSO)
j E Hawkins: *Modern Languages in the Curriculum*, 1981 (CUP)
k *Curriculum and Examinations in Secondary Schools* (Norwood Report), London, 1943 (HMSO)
l Angela Rumbold, JCLA, March 1987
m *Modern Studies* (Leathes Report), 1918 (HMSO)
n DES/Welsh Office: *Modern Languages in the School Curriculum: A Statement of Policy*, London, 1988 (HMSO)

References and notes

Chapter 1

1 DES: *Modern Foreign Languages to 16*, HMI Series: Curriculum Matters 8, p. 29, London, 1987 (HMSO)

2 E Hawkins: *Modern Languages in the Curriculum*, p. 67, Cambridge, 1987 (revised edition) (CUP)

3 Ibid., p. 63

4 C Burstall, M Jamieson, S Cohen and M Hargreaves: *Primary French in the Balance*, Slough, 1974 (NFER)

5 H Radford: 'Modern languages and the curriculum in English secondary schools', *Social Histories of the Secondary Curriculum*, ed. I F Goodson, p. 222, Lewes, 1985 (Falmer)

6 E Hawkins and G Lawrence: 'Modern language teachers: an endangered species', *Education*, p. 537, 24.6.88

7 P H Hoy: *The Early Teaching of Modern Languages*, London, 1977 (Nuffield Foundation)

8 Op. cit., H Radford, 1985; op. cit. E Hawkins, 1987

9 DES/Welsh Office: *Modern Languages in the School Curriculum: A Statement of Policy*, p. 2, London, 1988 (HMSO)

10 D Phillips: 'From Complacency to Conviction': thirty years of language teaching theory, practice and policy, in: *Languages in Schools*, ed. D Phillips London, 1988 (CILT)

11 Op. cit., DES/Welsh Office, 1988

12 Op. cit., H Radford, 1985

13 Ibid., p. 229

14 Ibid., p. 205

15 Ibid., p. 229

16 Op. cit., D Phillips, 1988, p. 6

17 Ibid., p. 7

18 B Rapaport and D Westgate: *Children Learning French*, London, 1974 (Methuen)

19 S Moore and A L Antrobus: *Audio-Visual French*, London, 1966 (Longman)

20 DES: *Modern Languages in Comprehensive Schools*, HMI Series: Matters for Discussion 3, London, 1977 (HMSO)

21 Assessment of Performance Unit (APU): *Report on 1984 survey of French*, London, 1986 (DES)

22 Op. cit., DES/Welsh Office, 1988, p. 4

23 Op. cit., H Radford, 1985, pp. 224–225

24 B Page and D Hewett: *Languages Step by Step: Graded Objectives in the UK*, London, 1988 (CILT)

25 Op. cit., D Phillips, 1988, p. 9

26 Op. cit., DES/Welsh Office, 1988, pp. 3–4

27 D Westgate, J Batey, J Brownlee and M Butler: 'Some characteristics of interaction in foreign language classrooms', *British Educational Research Journal*, Vol. 11, No. 3, 1985

28 C V James: 'Foreign languages in the school curriculum', *National Congress on Languages in Education*, Papers and Reports 1, ed. G Perren, London, 1979 (CILT)

29 Op. cit., E Hawkins, 1987, p. 80

30 Op. cit., C V James, p. 14

31 J Harzic: 'Le français et les autres langues de communication', *Une Langue: Le*

Français Aujourd'hui dans le Monde, eds. M Blancpain and A Rebouillet, p. 157, Paris, 1976 (Hachette)

32 R Woodhaugh: *Languages in Competition*, p. 141,Oxford, 1987 (Blackwell)

33 A Rebouillet: 'Images et réalités de la langue française', op. cit., p. 3, eds. M Blancpain and A Rebouillet, 1976

34 Op. cit., R Woodhaugh, 1987, p. 11

35 D Sanderson: *Modern Language Teachers in Action*, York, 1982 (University of York Language Teaching Centre)

36 DES: *Modern Languages in Comprehensive Schools*, HMI Series: Matters for Discussion 3, London, 1977 (HMSO)

37 R Mitchell: 'Process research in second language classrooms, *Language Teaching*, Vol. 18, No. 2, 1985

38 Op. cit., D Westgate et al., 1985

39 British Overseas Trade Board: *Foreign Languages for Overseas Trade*, 1979 (BOTB)

40 Op. cit., DES/Welsh Office, 1988, p. 2

41 D Embleton: 'Breaking barriers to international business competition', *British Journal of Language Teaching*, Vol. 26, No. 3, 1988

42 HMI: *An Inquiry into practice in 22 comprehensive schools where a foreign language forms part of the curriculum for all or almost all pupils up to age 16*, Report 292/87, London, 1987 (DES)

43 Ibid., p. 25

44 Ibid., p. 23

Chapter 2

1 C L Dodgson (Lewis Carroll): 'The Vision of the Three Ts'

2 G Faber: *Jowett*, London, 1957 (Faber & Faber)

3 *German Home Life*, p. 97, London, 1876 (Longmans, Green). I have described some of the difficulties which nineteenth-century travellers and others experienced with the language, in D Phillips: 'Problems with an Alien Tongue: the nineteenth-century traveller in Germany', *Modern Languages*, Vol. 70 No. 2, 1989

4 Reported in the *Western Morning News*, 2.9.18. I am grateful to Josefina Bello for drawing my attention to the text in question

5 The Leathes Report remains the only national report on language teaching

6 Board of Education: *Position of German in Grant-Aided Secondary Schools in England*, Educational Pamphlets No. 77, London, 1929 (HMSO)

7 *Curriculum and Examinations in Secondary Schools* (Norwood Report), p. 117, London, 1943 (HMSO)

8 Association of Teachers of German (ATG): 'German in Secondary Schools' p. 4, London, 1978

9 British Overseas Trade Board (BOTB): *Foreign Languages for Overseas Trade*, p. 20, London, 1979

10 D Phillips: 'From Complacency to Conviction': thirty years of language teaching theory, practice and policy, in: *Languages in Schools*, ed. D Phillips, p. 21, London, 1988 (CILT)

11 D Childs and A Noack: 'Commons, Bundestag: Survey Results Revealed', *Politics and Society in Germany, Austria and Switzerland*, pp. 7–8, Vol. 1, No. 1, Summer 1988

12 D Phillips (ed.): *Continuation German*, Oxford, 1978 (University of Oxford Department of Educational Studies)

13 Centre for Information on Language Teaching and Research (CILT): *German in the United Kingdom: Issues and Opportunities*, p. viii, London, 1986

14 D Crystal: *The Cambridge Encyclopedia of Language*, p. 287, Cambridge, 1987 (CUP)

15 Auswärtiges Amt der Bundesperublik Deutschland: *Die Stellung der deutschen Sprache in der Welt*, pp. 62–81, Bonn, 1985 (Bericht der Bundesregierung)

16 S Parkes: 'German: key language for Europe', *THES*, 1.12.78

17 Op. cit., Auswärtiges Amt, 1985, pp. 66–67

18 E Hawkins: *Modern Languages in the Curriculum*, Cambridge, 1984 (CUP)

19 D Phillips and C Filmer-Sankey: '*Vive la différence?* Some problems in investigating diversification of first foreign language provision in schools', *British Educational Research Journal*, Vol. 15, No. 3, 1989

20 A Keene: *German as Joint or Sole First Foreign Language in the Secondary School*, unpublished M.Sc dissertation, University of Oxford, 1980

21 M Tumber: 'Why German?', *TES*, 28.10.83

22 Assessment of Performance Unit (APU): *Foreign Language Performance in Schools. Report on 1983 survey of French, German and Spanish*, London, 1985 (DES, Department of Education for Northern Ireland, Welsh Office)

23 J Bello: *Spanish as First Foreign Language in Schools: Past and Present Perspectives*, OXPROD Occasional Paper 2, Oxford, 1989 (University of Oxford Department of Educational Studies)

24 F Johnson: *The German Mind*, p. 19, London and Sydney, 1922 (Chapman and Dodd)

25 D Phillips and V Stencel: *The Second Foreign Language: Past development, current trends and future prospects*, p. 46, London, 1983 (Hodder and Stoughton)

26 Ibid., p. 44

27 I have elsewhere (D Phillips, 1988, p. 8) paid tribute to the impact which *Vorwärts* had on German teaching from the late 1960s onwards. Its influence was widespread and beneficial

28 A Miller: *Second Foreign Languages in Oxfordshire Schools*, Oxford, 1980 (University of Oxford Department of Educational Studies)

29 V Stencel and D Phillips: *Second Foreign Language: An investigation into organisation, teaching methods and pupils' attitudes in Oxfordshire schools*, Oxford, 1982 (University of Oxford Department of Educational Studies); D Phillips: 'Teachers and "Second" Foreign languages: A Note on Methodology', *Modern Languages*, Vol. LXIV, No. 3, 1983

30 J Kapuste: 'Sprache und Realität in englischen Deutschlehrwerken', in: *The German Language Between Yesterday and Tomorrow*, E Kolinsky (ed.), p. 23, *Modern German Studies* No. 4, Birmingham, 1987 (Aston University)

31 Ibid., p. 25

32 R Davidson, pp. 79–80 in: CILT (1986), op. cit.

33 DES/Welsh Office: *Modern Languages in the School Curriculum: a Statement of Policy*, p. 8, London, 1988 (HMSO)

34 Her Majesty's Inspectorate (HMI): *An inquiry into practice in 22 comprehensive schools where a foreign language forms part of the curriculum for all or most pupils up to age 16*, Report 292/87, London, 1987 (DES)

35 James Russell Lowell, quoted in *The Golden Age of Travel*, ed. H. Barber Morrison, p. 132, London, 1953 (Andrew Melrose)

36 *Peanuts* (2633) © 1979

In addition to the works mentioned above, reference was also made to the following:

Centre for Information on Language Teaching and Research (CILT): *German in the United Kingdom: Problems and Prospects*, London, 1976

National Consortium for Examination Results (NCER): Examination Results, Summer 1988 Data (Consortium LEAs, Shire Counties, Metropolitan Districts & Outer London Boroughs)

Statistics of Education, Vol. 2 (School Leavers, CSE & GCE), London, 1973 (HMSO)

Chapter 3

1 T D Baldwin et al.: *Italian in Schools*, Papers from the Colloquium on the Teaching of Italian in the United Kingdom 1979, London, 1980 (CILT)
2 Data supplied by the Office of Population Censuses and Surveys
3 R C Powell: 'What gender is Italian?', *Journal of the Association of Teachers of Italian*, Vol. 27, 1979
4 DES/Welsh Office: *Modern Languages in the Curriculum: A Statement of Policy*, p. 8, London, 1988 (HMSO)
5 Op. cit., T D Baldwin et al., 1980, p. 25
6 G Mengon: *Emigrazione e lingua*, Padova, 1980 (Liviana Editrice)
7 Communicated to me directly by l'Ispettorato Didattico of the Italian Embassy, London
8 *Report of the Committee of Enquiry into the Education of Children from Ethnic Minority Groups*, pp. 702–703, London, 1985 (HMSO)
9 P Handley: *Adult Education and the Teaching of Languages: The Current Situation in England and Wales*, Brighton, 1984 (The Language Centre, Brighton Polytechnic)
10 Combined sales figures for the BBC Continuing Education coursebooks *Get By in Italian, Buongiorno Italia, L'Italia dal vivo*
11 R Andrews, S Hart: *Degree Course Guide 1988–89: Italian and Hispanic Studies*, Cambridge, 1988 (Hobsons Press)
12 P Hainsworth: 'Which future for Italian?', *Bulletin of the Society for Italian Studies*, 21, 1988
13 D Chaplin: 'Chronicle 1988', ibid.
14 Figures taken from the Graduate Teacher Training Registry's *Annual Statistical Survey*, 1988
15 Op. cit., T D Baldwin et al., 1980, pp. 89–93
16 Op. cit., DES/Welsh Office, 1988

Chapter 4

1 N Annan: *Report on the Teaching of Russian*, London, 1962 (HMSO)
2 Schools Council: *French in the Primary School*, Working Paper No. 8, London, 1966 (HMSO)
3 E Hawkins: *Modern Languages in the Curriculum*, Cambridge, 1981, (CUP)
4 D Phillips: 'From Complacency to Conviction: thirty years of language teaching, practice and policy', in: *Languages in Schools*, ed. D Phillips,London, 1988 (CILT)
5 DES/Welsh Office: *Modern Languages in the School Curriculum: A Statement of Policy*, London, 1988 (HMSO)
6 D Phillips and G Clark: *Attitudes Towards Diversification: Results of a Survey of Teacher Opinion*, OXPROD Occasional Paper No. 1, 1988

7 E Hawkins and G Lawrence, 'Modern language teachers – an endangered species', *Education*, 24.6.88
8 B P Pockney, 'The Case for Russian (or Russian is a key language in any future we may have)', inaugural lecture, University of Surrey, 1984
9 T Wade, 'Curtain Call', *TES* Modern Languages Extra, 25.11.88

Chapter 5

1 E Allison Peers: *Spanish – Now*, 1944 (Methuen)
2 DES/Welsh Office: *Modern Languages in the School Curriculum: A Statement of Policy*, 1988 (HMSO); DES: *Modern Foreign Languages to 16*, HMI Series: Curriculum Matters 8, London, 1987 (HMSO)
3 Ibid., p. 29
4 Association of Teachers of Spanish and Portuguese (ATSP): *Response*, 1987
5 DES: *The National Curriculum 5–16: A Consultation Document*, 1987 (HMSO)
6 Op. cit., E Allison Peers, 1944, p. vii
7 E Hawkins: *Modern Languages in the Curriculum*, 1987 (CUP)
8 Board of Education: Circular 797, p. 13, 1912
9 E Allison Peers (ed.): *A Handbook to the Study and Teaching of Spanish*, 1938 (Methuen)
10 Ibid., p. v
11 Ibid., p. vii
12 Modern Languages Association Report: *The Teaching of Spanish in Secondary Schools*, p. 40, 1936
13 Op. cit., E Allison Peers, 1944, p. 43
14 For a detailed treatment see D Phillips and V Stencel: *The Second Foreign Language*, 1983 (Hodder and Stoughton)
15 Op. cit., E Allison Peers, 1944, p. 43
16 S Rouve: *Where stands Spanish now?*, paper given at Annual Conference of the Association of Hispanists 1977, in *Vida Hispánica*, 1978
17 R Clarke: *The case for teaching Spanish in British Secondary Schools*, 1977 (ATSP)
18 See, in particular, publications of the Latin-American Trade Advisory Group
19 BOTB: *Foreign Languages for Overseas Trade*, London, 1979
20 Op. cit., E Hawkins, 1987, p. 43
21 DES: *Curriculum and Examinations in Secondary Schools*, 1943 (HMSO)
22 Chairman's opening address, reprinted in *Vida Hispánica*, Vol. 1, No. 4, 1947
23 Ibid., p. 13 (Teachers' Page)
24 Op. cit., E Allison Peers, 1944, p. v
25 *15 to 18*, 1959 (HMSO)
26 The Certificate of Secondary Education Examinations Bulletin No. 1, 1963 (HMSO)
27 Extracts from issues of *Vida Hispánica* 1961, 1962; 1963 XI, 3, p. 27: *CSE*, M C M Roberts; 1964 XII, 2 & 3, B Dutton; 1964 XII, I, *The Teaching of Spanish; 1965 XIII*, 2, pp. 11–22; 1968 XVI, 2, pp. 15–16, D Utley: Spanish in a *Comprehensive School*
28 SCMLP: *Report on the Teaching of Spanish in UK Schools: Stands Spanish where it should?* 1972
29 *Vida Hispánica*, 1971, XIX, 3, p. 3. Letter from Professor F W Pierce
30 Mention must be made of the outstanding work of TASC, Leeds, and the LTC, York, but, across the UK, this hardly counts as planned provision

31 HMI: *Modern Languages in Comprehensive Schools*, HMI Series: Matters for Discussion 3, 1977 (HMSO)
32 Ibid., p. 32
33 ILEA: *Foreign Languages in Comprehensive Schools*, 1978
34 Rouve and Ingamells (eds.): *The Spanish Colloquium*, p. 2, 1979 (CILT)
35 Op. cit., DES 1987; op. cit., DES/Welsh Office, 1988
36 See, for instance, papers in Section 1 of *The Spanish Colloquium*, 1978: A Hitchens, 'Spanish as a First Foreign language'; G Mathie: 'Teaching Spanish as a Second Foreign Language'
37 D Phillips and G Clark: *Attitudes Towards Diversification*, OXPROD Occasional Paper 1, p. 1, 1988 (University of Oxford Department of Educational Studies)
38 NALA: *Foreign Languages in Schools* (undated pamphlet)
39 C G Hadley (ed.): *Languages other than French in the Secondary School*, 1981 (Schools Council)
40 Ibid., pp. 26–27
41 Op. cit., D Phillips and V Clark, 1988
42 Ibid., pp. 13, 15, 17
43 Op. cit., DES/Welsh Office, 1988, p. 9
44 ATSP: *Survey of the Teaching of Spanish in England, Wales and Scotland 1984*, D G Thomas, 1984 (ATSP-Wolverhampton Polytechnic)
45 R Goulden: 'Alternative Sources of Supply of Teachers of Spanish', paper in Section 3 of *The Spanish Colloquium 1978*; see also: op. cit., *Modern Languages in the School Curriculum: A Statement of Policy*, DES/Welsh Office, 1988
46 F Rees *Languages for a Change*, 1989 (NFER-Nelson)
47 Ibid., p. 33
48 For example, the ten-week Spanish INSET course at King's College, London, taught jointly in the Spanish and Education Departments
49 'Europa 2000', *El País, Suplemento de Educación*, 24.1.89
50 ATSP: Response to MLISC, 1984
51 B Parr: 'Modern Languages for the Majority', *NALA Journal*, 1973
52 Op. cit., E Allison Peers, 1944, p. 92
53 ATSP: *Coloquio 40: Proceedings*, 1989; 'Diversification' (special issue) *Vida Hispánica*, Spring 1988
54 S Rouve: 'Spanish: the realistic alternative', *TES*, 13.11.87

Chapter 6

1 Rosen and Burgess: *Languages and Dialects of London School Children*, London, 1980 (Ward Lock Education)
2 Linguistic Minorities Project (LMP): *The Other Languages of Britain*, London, 1985 (RKP)
3 J Bourne: *Moving into Mainstream*, 1989 (NFER-Nelson)
4 F Turner: *Results of Mother Tongue Language Survey*, Oxford, 1986 (Internal Report, Oxfordshire County Council)
5 DES: *The Education of Immigrants*, Circular 7/65, London (HMSO)
6 J Miller: 'The School in a Multicultural Society', *Many Voices Bilingualism, Culture and Education*, 1980 (RKP)
7 DES: *Education Act*, London, 1944 (HMSO)
8 CRE: *Ethnic Minority Community Languages*, London, 1979

References and notes

9 DES: *Education in Schools*, London, 1977 (HMSO)
10 DES: *A Language for Life* (Bullock Report), London, 1975 (HMSO)
11 European Commission: *Directive on the Education of the Children of Migrant Workers*, Circular 77/86, Brussels, 1977 (EC)
12 DES: *Directive of the Council of the European Community on the Education of Migrant Workers*, London, 1981
13 DES: Circular 5/81
14 DES: *Education for All* (Swann Report), London, 1985
15 DES: *Foreign Languages in the School Curriculum*, London, 1986 (HMSO)
16 DES/Welsh Office: *Modern Languages in the School Curriculum: A Statement of Policy*, London, 1988 (HMSO)
17 Op. cit., J Bourne, 1989
18 Information from the Adviser for Bilingualism, Birmingham, 1989
19 DES: *Report of the Committee of Enquiry into the Teaching of English Language* (Kingman Report), London, 1988 (HMSO)
20 DES: *English for Ages 5–11 National Curriculum Working Party* (Cox Report) London, 1988 (HMSO)
21 Op. cit., DES/Welsh Office, 1988
22 Ibid.
23 Ibid.
24 Ibid.
25 Ibid.
26 Ibid.
27 Ibid.

Chapter 7

1 *Educational Report*, Part 3, p. 59, 1847
2 *Educational Report*, Part 1, p. iii, 1847
3 *Report of the Commission of Inquiry into the State of Education in Wales*, Part 2, London, 1847
4 Reverend D J Davies: 'The Necessity of Teaching English through the Medium of Welsh', *Y Cymmrodor*, Vol. V, pp. 1–13, 1882
5 V Morgan: *The Life and Sayings of Kilsby Jones*, London, 1896
6 Gittins: *Primary Education in Wales*, London, 1967 (HMSO); H Giles (ed.): *Language, Ethnicity, and Intergroup Relations*, London, 1977 (Academic Press)
7 Welsh Office: *Statistics of Education in Wales: Schools, 1987*, No. 1, Cardiff, 1988
8 M Griffiths (ed.): *The Welsh Language in Education*, Cardiff, 1986 (WJEC)
9 *Reports – Adroddiadau 1987–1988*, Cardiff (University of Wales)
10 Gwynedd LEA: *Gwynedd Language Policy Document*, 1987 (Gwynedd County Council)
11 P M Rawkins: *The Implementation of Language Policy in the Schools of Wales*, 1979 (Centre for the Study of Public Policy, University of Strathclyde)
12 J Aitchison and H Carter: *The Welsh Language 1961–1981. An Interpretive Atlas*, Cardiff, 1985
13 Welsh Office: *Welsh in the Primary Schools of Gwynedd, Powys and Dyfed*, Welsh Education Survey No. 5, Cardiff, 1977
14 DES/Welsh Office: *National Curriculum: Welsh Working Group Interim Report*, p. 3, November 1988

15 Made available by the Welsh Office
16 Op. cit., DES/Welsh Office, 1988, p. 10
17 Para. 13.5; DES/Welsh Office, *English* for ages 5 to 16, June 1989 (HMSO)
18 B McLaughlin: *Theories of Second-Language Learning*, p. 206, London, 1987 (Edward Arnold)
19 S Krashen and T Terrell: *The Natural Approach: Language Acquisition in the Classroom*, 1983 (Alemany Press)
20 Op. cit., DES/Welsh Office, 1988, p. 15
21 Ibid., p. 10
22 Ibid., p. 43
23 Ibid., pp. 7, 16, 17, 44
24 H Giles (ed.): *Language, Ethnicity and Intergroup Relations*, London, 1977 (Academic Press); Harrison, Bellin and Piette: *Bilingual Mothers and the Language of their Children*, Cardiff, 1981 (University of Wales Press)
25 C Burstall et al.: *Primary French in the Balance*, Slough, 1974 (NFER)
26 Op. cit., Welsh Office, 1977, p. 24
27 Op. cit., DES/Welsh Office, 1988, p. 53
28 Ibid., p. 11
29 Ibid., p. 43
30 Ibid.
31 Op. cit., p. 65
32 Op. cit., Gwynedd LEA, 1987, p. 1

Chapter 8

1 See, for example, S Hagen: 'German – the First Foreign Language of Northern English Industry', *German in the United Kingdom: Issues and Opportunities*, London, 1986 (CILT); D Embleton: 'Breaking Barriers to International Business Communication', *British Journal of Language Teaching*, Vol. 26, No. 3, 1988; E Hawkins: *Modern Languages in the Curriculum* (revised edition), Cambridge, 1987 (CUP)
2 See, for example, C G Hadley et al.: *Languages other than French in the Secondary School*, London, 1981 (Schools Council); D Phillips and G Clark: *Attitudes towards Diversification Results of a Survey of Teacher Opinion*, OXPROD Occasional Paper 1, Oxford, 1988 (University of Oxford Department of Educational Studies)
3 Op. cit., E Hawkins: 1987, p. 78
4 C V James: 'Foreign languages in the school curriculum', *Foreign Languages in Education*, NCLE Papers and Reports 1, 1978
5 Op. cit., E Hawkins, 1987, p. 82
6 H Sweet: *A Practical Study of Languages*, London, 1899 (Dent)
7 Op. cit., E Hawkins, 1987, p. 80
8 Ibid., pp. 81–82
9 E A Hopkins: 'Contrastive Analysis, Interlanguage and the Learner', in: W F W Lohnes and E A Hopkins: *The Contrastive Grammar of English and German*, Michigan, 1982 (Karoma)
10 Op. cit., E Hawkins, 1987, p. 82
11 Ibid., p. 83
12 Ibid, p. 84
13 Ibid., p. 85
14 A E Keene: *German as Joint or Sole First Foreign Language in the Secondary School*,

unpublished M.Sc. dissertation, University of Oxford, 1984
15 W M Rivers: *A Practical Guide to the Teaching of French*, New York, 1975 (OUP)
16 Op. cit., A E Keene, 1984
17 J Bello: *Spanish as a First Foreign Language in British Schools: Past Development and Present Practice*, unpublished Special Diploma dissertation, Oxford, 1988
18 Op. cit., E Hawkins, 1987, p. 83
19 K Breul: *The Teaching of Modern Languages and the Training of Teachers* (fourth edition), pp. 78–79, Cambridge, 1913 (CUP)
20 H L Kufner: *The Grammatical Structures of English and German*, p. 9, Chicago, 1962 (University of Chicago Press)
21 Op. cit., J Bello, 1988, p. 30
22 Op. cit., E Hawkins, 1987, p. 87
23 Op. cit., W M Rivers, 1975, p. 170; W M Rivers, K M Dell 'Orto and V J Dell 'Orto: *A Practical Guide to the Teaching of German*, pp. 170–172, New York, 1975 (OUP)
24 W Rippmann: *Hints on Teaching German*, p. 7, London, 1906 (Dent)
25 Op. cit., H L Kufner, 1962, pp. 75–76
26 Op. cit., J Bello, 1988, p. 41
27 Op. cit., H Sweet, 1899, p. 54
28 Op. cit., E A Hopkins, 1982, p. 48
29 M Tumber: 'German as First Foreign Language', *German in the United Kingdom: Issues and Opportunities*, p. 45, London, 1986 (CILT)
30 D Phillips and V Stencel: *The Second Foreign language: Past developments, current trends and future prospects*, p. 46, London, 1983 (Hodder and Stoughton)
31 A Miller: *Report on the Pre-testing of a Language Aptitude Test*, BP Modern Languages Project Occasional Paper 1, p. 39, Oxford, 1980 (University of Oxford Department of Educational Studies)
32 Assessment of Performance Unit (APU): *Foreign Language Performance in Schools. Report on 1983 survey of French, German and Spanish*, 1985 (DES/Department of Education for Northern Ireland/Welsh Office); (APU): *Foreign Language Performance in Schools. Report on 1984 survey of French*, 1986 (DES/Department of Education for Northern Ireland/Welsh Office); APU: Foreign *Language Performance in Schools. Report on 1985 survey of French*, London, 1987 (HMSO)
33 Op. cit., APU, 1985, p. 394
34 See, for example, op. cit., A E Keene, 1984; op. cit., M Tumber, 1986; D Phillips and G Clark, 1988; C Filmer-Sankey: *A Study of First-Year Pupils' Attitudes towards French, German and Spanish*, OXPROD Occasional Paper 3, Oxford, 1989 (University of Oxford Department of Educational Studies)
35 R C Gardner and W E Lambert: *Attitudes and Motivation in Second Language Learning*, 1972, Massachusetts (Newbury House)
36 C Burstall et al.: *Primary French in the Balance*, 1974, Windsor (NFER)
37 Ibid.
38 Ibid., p. 244
39 H H Stern: *Fundamental Concepts of Language Teaching*, Oxford, 1983 (OUP); S Krashen: *Second Language Acquisition and Second Language Learning*, Oxford, 1981 (Pergamon Press)
40 Op. cit., S Krashen, 1981, p. 5
41 Op. cit., H H Stern, 1983, p. 385
42 Op. cit., APU,1985
43 Ibid., p. 390

44 Ibid., p. 391
45 M Buckby et al.: *Graded objectives and tests for modern languages; an evaluation*, London, 1981 (Schools Council)
46 Op. cit., APU, 1985, 1986 and 1987
47 Op. cit., C Filmer-Sankey, 1989
48 Op. cit., APU, 1985, p. 391
49 Ibid.
50 *Bibliobus* (Mary Glasgow Publications Ltd., 1983 and 1984) is a reading library in three stages for learners of French
51 All first-year pupils learning French in the OXPROD project schools use *Tricolore 1* by S Honner, R Holt and H Mascie-Taylor, published in 1984 (revised edition) by Arnold-Wheaton

Chapter 9

1 DES: *Modern Languages in Comprehensive Schools*, HMI Series: Matters for Discussion 3, London, 1977 (HMSO)
2 DES/Welsh Office: *Modern Languages in the School Curriculum: A Statement of Policy*, London, 1988 (HMSO)
3 F Rees: *Languages for a Change*, 1989 (NFER-Nelson)
4 Ibid., p. 39
5 In Year 1 of the project each authority was given £30,000 to pay for coordinators to select approximately ten schools in each authority. In Year 2 £50,000 was given to each: £30,000 for materials and £20,000 for INSET. This latter figure was raised by virement to £27,500. In Year 3 £4,300,000 is to be given to all the LEAs. It is interesting to note that Lancashire has little experience of diversification. Only 2½ schools had diversified prior to the introduction of the pilot scheme.
6 Paired intensive days involve pairs of teachers working with a Spanish or German tutor for intensive 'days', from 9 a.m. to 9 p.m. This is a model used by the College for companies such as ICI and British Aerospace. They will be tailored to individual needs but will generally be at an advanced level. These days would take place on 'Baker days' or weekends. This is a new initiative which has to date not been tried.
7 Lancashire can also take advantage of the INSET programmes arranged by the Goethe-Institut and the newly founded Spanish Institute in Manchester. Both put on courses for language study (as well as providing methodological support for teachers) and the German and Spanish Institutes offer examinations at different levels.
8 Op. cit., F Rees, 1989 pp. 54–55
9 The mapping instrument has been used by a number of LEAs as an initial step in identifying schools which might be able to diversify. Copies of the instrument are available from CILT.
10 Op. cit., DES/Welsh Office, 1988
11 DES: *Modern foreign languages to 16*, HMI Series: Curriculum Matters 8, London, 1987 (HMSO)

Chapter 10

1 DES/Welsh Office: *Modern Languages in the School Curriculum: A Statement of Policy*, 1988 (HMSO)
2 K Fenwick and P McBride: *The Government of Education in Britain*, p. 32, 1981 (Martin Robertson)

3 DES: *Foreign Languages in the School Curriculum: A Consultative Paper*, London, 1983 (HMSO)

4 DES: *Foreign Languages in the School Curriculum: A Draft Statement of Policy*, London, 1986 (HMSO)

5 Assessment of Performance Unit (APU): *Foreign Language Provision, Survey of Schools, Autumn 1982*, Occasional Paper No. 2, 1983 (DES); APU: *Foreign Language Performance in Schools, Report on the 1983 Survey of French, German and Spanish*, 1985 (DES); APU: *Foreign Language Performance in Schools, Report on the 1984 Survey of French*, 1986 (DES)

6 Schools Council: *Languages other than French in the secondary school: an exploratory study of other languages as first or equal first language* (Hadley Report), *1981:* Schools Council Modern Languages Committee: *The Second Foreign Language in Secondary Schools: a question of survival*, Spring 1982

7 DES: *Boys and Modern Languages*, 1985 (HMSO); DES: *An inquiry into practice in 22 comprehensive schools where a foreign language forms part of the curriculum for all or almost all pupils up to age 16*, 1987 (HMSO); DES: *Modern Languages to 16*, Curriculum Matters 8, 1987 (HMSO)

8 Op. cit., DES, 1985

9 Ibid., Para. 120

10 Leathes Report, *Report of the Committee appointed by the Prime Minister to enquire into the position of Modern Languages in the educational system of Great Britain*, 1918 (HMSO)

11 Ibid. p. 92

12 Ibid. p. 228

13 Ibid. pp. 228–9

14 Op. cit., Schools Council, 1981

15 Ibid., p. 10

16 It is this hypothesis which much of the research at OXPROD sets out to explore

17 The results of a survey conducted by OXPROD in 1988, as yet unpublished, indicate that this situation still obtains in spite of frequent calls from the DES that LEAs should draw up clear statements of policy for implementation in maintained schools

18 This recommendation has been ignored in *Modern Languages in the Curriculum*, where a fourth year start is proposed for the second foreign language to avoid breaching the common curriculum. For further discussion of the advisability of French as a joint first language, see D Phillips and G Clark: *Attitudes towards Diversification. Results of a survey of teacher opinion*, OXPROD Occasional Paper 1, Oxford, 1988 (University of Oxford Department of Educational Studies)

19 Criterion referencing introduced with GCSE should alleviate this problem

20 Op. cit., DES 1983

21 *The Secondary School Curriculum and Examinations: with special reference to the 14 to 16 year old age group*, House of Commons Second Report from the Education, Science and Arts Committee, Session 1981–1982, Vol. 1, 16.12.81 (HMSO)

22 Op. cit., DES, 1983

23 The question of the feasibility of staffing a language for all pupils through to age 16 as part of the National Curriculum, whether French or any other language, remains unresolved. The secondary heads and other professional bodies have estimated that between 3,000 and 4,000 extra modern language teachers would be needed to deliver the National Curriculum, and these estimates are based on teacher training institutions meeting their current targets. The National Foundation for Educational

Research (NFER) has undertaken a study to ascertain what untapped capacity to teach languages other than French currently exists in the teaching profession, and their results have been published in F Rees: *Languages for a Change*, 1989 (NFER-Nelson). Concern that staffing will be a major problem is widespread, as evidenced in frequent reports in the professional journals and in the media generally

24 This statement appears to ignore the fact that of all the areas in which teachers of foreign languages feel the need for particular confidence and competence, especially when their skills have not been recently put to use, oral work figures particularly highly. See op. cit., David Phillips and Georgina Clark, 1988

25 See note 21 above

26 Op. cit., DES, 1986, Para. 1

27 In March 1989 the Secretary of State announced that maintained schools will be required to offer at least one of the working languages of the European Community – Danish, Dutch, French, German, Modern Greek, Italian, Portuguese or Spanish. As David Phillips points out, however, in his Introduction to this volume, this choice of languages owes more to political expediency than to educational considerations or indeed practical feasibility

28 Thus in 1973 the authors of a guide to parents explained:

Broadly speaking, the Secretary of State has a regulating function, laying down rules about standards of provision and setting the context in which local education authorities work. The initiative for planning and providing education rests not with central government but with local authorities

J Pratt, T Burgess, R Allemano, M Locke: *Your Local Education*, p. 39f, 1973 (Penguin)

29 DES: *Local Authority Arrangements for the School Curriculum*, November 1979 (HMSO)

30 DES: *Foreign Languages in the School Curriculum: A Draft Statement of Policy*, Para. *40*, June 1986

31 The LEAs in question are, in alphabetical order, Avon, Birmingham, Bolton, Buckinghamshire, Croydon, Essex, Hampshire, Havering, Lancashire and Staffordshire. Interim reports on their respective pilot projects are available from CILT.

32 Responses from LEAs with middle schools included the following:

One problem here is that middle schools teach French – and it would be unrealistic to expect them to be able to offer an alternative FL. This has implications affecting the possibility of diversification in high schools. (One high school has in some years received an intake from as many as 37 different middle schools.)

One of our main problems is the middle school situation in which all middle schools begin French at the age of 10 and therefore with the transfer sometimes at 12 and sometimes 13 continuity of foreign language provision would be difficult other than in French.